Have a Nice Birthday

Love, _ _ _ _ _

TOUGH
GUY

TOUGH GUY

GUY BY ALLEN GARR

Bill Bennett and the
taking of British Columbia

KEY PORTER BOOKS

Copyright © 1985 by Allen Garr

Canadian Cataloguing in Publication Data

Garr, Allen, 1941-
  Tough guy : Bill Bennett and the taking of
British Columbia

Bibliography: p.
Includes index.
ISBN 0-919493-77-7

1. Bennett, W.R. (William Richards), 1932-
2. Prime ministers – British Columbia – Biography.
3. British Columbia – Politics and government –
1975-   *I. Title.

FC3828.1.B46G37 1985   971.1'04'0924   C85-099718-6
F1088.B46G37 1985

"It Couldn't Be Done"
Reprinted from *The Collected Verse of Edgar A. Guest*
© 1934 with permission of Contemporary Books, Inc., Chicago.

Key Porter Books Limited
70 The Esplanade
Toronto, Ontario
Canada M5E 1R2

Cover Design: William Fox/Associates
Design: Joanna Gertler
Typesetting: Computer Composition
Printing and Binding: John Deyell Company
Printed and bound in Canada

85 86 87 88 6 5 4 3 2 1

Contents

For Megan and Sarah

Acknowledgements

My thanks to friends and fellow journalists who allowed me to rifle their files, pick their brains, and raid their libraries to write this book. In particular Joan Andersen, Pat Annesley, Cameron Bell, Keith Bradbury, Clem Chapple, Russ Clifford, Peter Comparelli, Russ Froese, John Gibbs, Steve Hume, Pamela Martin, Barbara McLintock, Rod Mickleburgh, Ian Mulgrew, John Sawatsky, Dan Smith, Eli Sopow, Harvey Southam, Sarah Spinks, Ben Tierney, Dave Todd, Sharon Vance, Wayne Williams, and Lorne Mallin, whose assistance with research was invaluable.

Gerald Haslam, Publisher of the Vancouver *Sun* and *The Province*, allowed me access to the Pacific Press Library where librarians Shirley Mooney, Barbara Valle, and their staff, were helpful as always. Victoria legislative librarian Maureen Lawson put up with my many questions, as did librarians and clerks at the Metro Toronto Library and the Vancouver Public Library. MP Jim Fulton and his Ottawa staff were kind and generous with their time and office space.

Joan Andersen, Kelly Crichton, Lorne Mallin, Alan Merridew, Rod Mickleburgh, Craig Paterson, Judy Scolnik, Mel Watkins, and Bob Waller waded through early drafts of the manuscript and were refreshingly brutal in their criticism. Charis Wahl cheered me up through the bleakness of an Ontario winter and attacked the text with an editorial knife as sharp and precise as her wit. Leo McGrady kindly read the galleys and saved me from myself.

Many people agreed to be interviewed for this book either on or off the record, briefly or at length. Those who did not precede their remarks with, "Just make sure my name or any reference to me doesn't turn up in the damned book," include Richard Allen, Cliff Andstein, Tom Axworthy, Richard Bassett, David Brown, Larry Bell, Vandy Britton, Jean Chrétien, John Fryer, Colin Gablemann, Martin Goldfarb, Peter Gusen, Bill Hamilton, Mike Harcourt, George Hewison, Bruce Howe, Stephen Kelleher, Bill Knight, Mike Kramer, Mark Krasnick, Art Kube, Larry Kuehn, Jerry Lampert, Gary Lauk, Clive Lyttle, Jim Matkin, Pat McGeer, Ian McKinnon, David Mitchell, Jack Munro, Ray Perrault, Jim Pattison, Stan Persky, Stephen Rogers, Gerry Scott, Renate Shearer, Gerry Stoney, Hugh Segal, Bob Skelly, Michael Walker, Frances Wasserlein, and Mel Watkins. The others know who they are.

Notes from the War Zone

It is Friday, July 8, 1983. Bill Bennett's government has just unleashed one of the most radical programs for social and economic change to hit the western world since the Second World War. British Columbia has suddenly become the testing ground for a neo-conservative ideology more pervasive than Thatcher's in Britain, less constrained than Reagan's in America. The neo-conservative drum has sounded from the bunker of the Fraser Institute for almost a decade and has found its cadence in the works of Adam Smith, Milton Friedman and Mancur Olson. While Bennett attacks, an international school of economic thought is developing around his offensive in British Columbia. This is the war for less, the war for restraint. The opening shot will be heard throughout the continent.

The Socred transition team moves with military precision to terminate twenty-one workers in the Human Rights Branch, where human rights legislation is enforced, and in the Human Rights Commission, which performs an educational role. In Victoria, senior bureaucrat Bob Plecas tells journalists that firings will be sensitive and not "draconian". With orders from Victoria and a command post at the ministry of labour offices in Burnaby, hit men fan out across the province. Seven regional Human Rights

Branch offices are shut down on Friday, and the locks are changed.

Ken Chamberlain is a Socred flunkey. (He also appears on TV, chubby, grinning, balding and waist-deep in a bathtub, playing with a yellow, rubber fish for the greater glory of Pharmasave Drugs Ltd.) July 8, 1983, is his finest hour.

Two women are at their desks when Chamberlain enters the Vancouver office of the Human Rights Commission. One is researcher Barbara Binns, a black Jamaican who has worked for the commission for the past year. The other is Doris Hall, a middle-aged Winnipeger, eighteen months on staff. Chamberlain, a total stranger to them, hands them termination notices and gives them fifteen minutes to clear out their desks, take their personal belongings, hand over their office keys and get out.

In Victoria, tall, blond Bert Hick, the angular, middle-management minion responsible for the Human Rights Branch, has tears in his eyes. It is his job to tell the workers at head office that they have been culled. The Human Rights Branch director, Hanne Jensen, finds out that her nine-year career with the B.C. public service is over only after the legislation is introduced in the House. Her workers are being fired and she is isolated from the power centre. Finally she, too, will be terminated.

Twenty-four hours later a government agent is on the prowl for human rights worker Peter Threlfell. Threlfell is at home in Kamloops with friends and family celebrating his birthday when the knock comes at his door. He is given a letter signed by the acting deputy minister of labour that tells him he is "redundant". The agent demands Threlfell's credit cards and the keys to his office and the government car. If he wants to retrieve personal effects from the office, he will have to be escorted and supervised by the agent. "I had a dream," Threlfell confesses a few days later, "that I was in prewar Germany."

Sunday morning, July 10. Human rights worker Ross Fedy is at home with his daughter in Usk, north-east of Terrace. For the past five years Ross Fedy has worked as a human rights officer, first in Prince George, then in Terrace. Before that he was an administrator with the federal government.

Most recently he handled the precedent-setting case of one Bhupinder Singh Dhaliwal, whom Plateau Mills had refused to hire on the grounds that he couldn't speak English.

Now government agent Dan Martin is at Fedy's door. He got this far with the help of the RCMP after being on Fedy's trail for three days. Sergeant Lablonde in Terrace did not know Fedy's whereabouts, but he directed agent Martin to a local parole officer, Rob Watts. Finally, putting bits and pieces together, Martin ended up in Usk.

The agent gives Fedy his redundancy notice. As he hands over his credit cards, office keys, and car keys, Fedy reads the notice, which says: "You will continue to be paid your regular salary up to and including October 31, 1983. And between now and that date, if requested, you will be expected to report to work in order to assist in the orderly transition." Agent Martin realizes he can't move both Fedy's car and his own back to Terrace. He departs, returns shortly with his family, and drives off in Fedy's vehicle, leaving his wife to manage the Martins' car.

Labour Minister Bob McClelland says that this firing procedure is being used out of concern for the human rights workers. McClelland wanted to save his employees the pain of finding out through the news media.

At 8:45 A.M. on Monday, July 11, Ken Chamberlain advances on the commission offices in Vancouver to establish his beachhead. "I'm just following orders," Chamberlain explains. Human rights commissioner Renate Shearer resists, holds her post, and chain-smokes until she is joined by commission chairman Charles Paris, whose good and faithful workers were given fifteen minutes by Chamberlain to pack their bags and get out.

Paris draws himself up to his full five feet four inches and sneers, "I'm still chairman of the Human Rights Commission." Chamberlain backs off. "I'm just a messenger boy. My orders are just to sit here, and I don't know why." Paris advances. "We will be having a commission meeting here now, and I'm not sure I'd be willing to let you hear what this commission has to discuss."

Chamberlain phones the Burnaby command post. "Hi, it's your old friend again. Mr. Paris wants me to leave. Shall I leave? Fine, I'll do that." As he walks out, he turns and says, "It's hell, but somebody has to do it."

The postman comes by the open door and is puzzled. "I was told not to deliver any mail here after Friday."

1
WACKY

In the clean, moist cool of an Alberta June, Wacky and May
Bennett load the car up with their youngsters, Anita and
R.J., and all the supplies they'll need for a few months on
the road. As they head south out of the village of Clyde on
their way to the West Coast, their small vehicle seems
wafted along by lush, green fields of grain that roll to every
horizon. It is 1930. Alberta is just starting to feel the sharp
bite of the Depression. Wheat, the spine of the provincial
economy, is about to take a beating on the world market.
Wacky has sold off his hardware business to his partner at a
fair profit and has locked up the house. It's time to move
on.

William Andrew Cecil Bennett. When he was a lad his
friends called him Cecil. When he jumped into politics
some people referred to him as W.A.C. Almost everybody
called him Wacky.

Wacky Bennett first came to these parts because of his
father, Andy, a brawling, drifting, no-account man who
never held down a job and had even less interest in holding
together a family. After some active duty in the First World
War, Andy Bennett left his wife and children in precarious
New Brunswick poverty and hopped a train west. His plan
was to pick up some Alberta Peace River farmland set aside
for veterans. Bury the past.

Eighteen-year-old Wacky, the youngest child, travelled
with this father he hardly knew, bringing with him his life

savings of $100 dollars, a few years' experience clerking in a
Saint John hardware store, a taste for Tory politics, and a
Presbyterian thirst for work, clean living, and God – a thirst
acquired from his long-suffering mother, Mary Emma. He
would have nothing to do with his father's fallen ways and
joined his mother, sister Olivia, and brother Russell when
they arrived in Edmonton in a fruitless attempt at a family
reconciliation. Wacky found work at Marshall Wells, the
hardware merchants. He spent many of his summer early
mornings in vigorous games of tennis and his evenings and
Sundays in Christian pursuits. He didn't smoke. He didn't
drink. And he wouldn't be caught dead in a dance hall.

His social life was bounded by Christian youth groups,
and it was through one such group, meeting in the basement of an Edmonton church, that he first encountered his
future wife, a tall, slender school teacher three years his
senior. Annie Elizabeth May Richards was a Presbyterian of
British stock and a British Columbia native.

When he wasn't courting May or weighing out pounds of
nails, Wacky took correspondence courses in business
management and was self-taught in the Power of Positive
Thinking School of Simple Solutions. Edgar A. Guest's
poem "It Couldn't Be Done" became his morning anthem,
bellowed at the top of his lungs before he bounced down to
breakfast:

> Somebody said that it couldn't be done
> But he with a chuckle replied
> That "maybe it couldn't," but he would be one
> Who wouldn't say no till he'd tried.
> So he buckled right in with a trace of a grin
> On his face. If he worried he hid it.
> He started to sing as he tackled the thing
> That couldn't be done, and he did it.

His well-thumbed copy of Dr. Orison Swett Marden's
Pushing to the Front would later be conspicuous in the
Bennett household – like some primer on the facts of life –
to be stumbled upon by his young children.

The Bennetts' 1930 car journey to the coast was arduous. There were no highways connecting Alberta and B.C.; the only route was down through Montana, across the Rockies into Washington, and then north again. Stunning beauty, rotten roads. The family's destination was a small cottage in Victoria owned by May's aunt. Within a week Wacky was vacationed out. While the wife and kiddies stayed at the cottage he headed over to Vancouver and then into the southern interior of B.C., looking for a new business. Something in a small town, a good place to raise a family.

Four days out he came to the Okanagan Valley and the town of Kelowna, a small agricultural community on a long lake that runs between high sage-covered plateaus. Population just shy of 5,000. David Leckie, an aging Scot, had an established hardware store for sale, one of the town's biggest businesses. They cut a deal: sixty-eight cents on the dollar for the inventory plus a two-story building on the main street.

Wacky packed up the family one last time and headed off to rented quarters and a failing Valley economy. While May raised the kids, Wacky downsized his inventory, clearing out the junk. He held the first sale in the store's history. He trimmed and clipped and hustled, and he ended up with $30,000 in cash. "The finest music in the country," he crooned, "is the ringing of cash registers." Bad times, he would conclude, are the best times to start a business. You learn prudence and have an eye for the bottom line.

In the midst of all this enterprise, the Bennetts' third and last child came into the world on April 14, 1932. William Richards Bennett was a frail, jaundiced baby with an array of allergies that would plague him for years. By the time Billy was born, Wacky's church activities were being subsumed by a commitment to his business and a growing involvement in the politics of a small town. Wacky also continued to nurture his fetish about debt – throughout the Depression he resisted the temptation to sign a bank loan – and this aversion to deficits, like his push-button homilies, his passion for commerce, and his devotion to the power of positive thinking would be his legacy to his children and to the province.

The Depression that nudged Wacky Bennett out of Alberta threw the provincial government, the United Farmers of Alberta, into a frantic search for solutions to a collapsing world wheat market and crippling bank debt that were driving people off the land. The economic theories of a British-based engineer named Major Clifford Hugh Douglas caught the government's attention and the impoverished province's imagination. In 1935 Douglas was invited to address a special legislative committee. He called his theory Social Credit. He presented a mathematical formula: the "A plus B Theorem", one part algebra and three parts snake oil.

The Douglas system claimed that it could put a lid on prices and redress the balance between consumers and producers by issuing scrip, putting money back in the hands of the people – social credit. His critics called it "funny money". It was an economic theory that would never be put into practice, much less understood; but Social Credit branches popped up across the West like mushrooms after a rain. Douglas served up a dish that satisfied the tastes of an uncommonly broad and loony bunch including, among others, the British Israel World Federation, or British Israelites. British Israelites are a fading lot in Canada now, but in their heyday, around the Second World War, they would pack Toronto's Massey Hall for rallies. They are fierce British Loyalists and Christian fundamentalists with a bottom-line view of biblical teachings.

They also believe they are part of the ten lost tribes of Israel, a proposition that puts them on a collision course with Jews. (British Israelites complain that Jews get all the glory of being "chosen" when British Israelites are God's chosen people, too.) They take a biblical approach to the evil of usury – charging interest on loans; usury is decried in a dozen places in the Old Testament alone, from Exodus to Ecclesiastes. In the 1930s some among them held that the evil banks of Wall Street were controlled by Jews. Douglas in his later ravings wrote about "Dark Forces" and a plot by

Jewish financiers to enslave the industrialized world. These were the anti-Semitic roots that allowed James Keegstra, a latter-day Alberta Social Crediter, to thrive.

The anti-Semitic option was, however, a fringe attraction, and the appeal of Social Credit for the United Farmers was slightly more rational. Social Credit preached a "non-partisan" cure for the world's economic woes, to rid us all of poverty. (In the West, non-partisan ultimately stood for anti-socialist or anti-communist; definitely for free enterprise. The Vancouver civic party, which was formed in the 1930s to hold the CCF at bay, called itself the Non-Partisan Association and operated from the 1950s onward as a B.C. Socred civic farm team.) The United Farmers were elected as a rejection of the partisan politics of the old-line Liberals and Tories. As well, they had a natural aversion, shared by most western Canadians, to those money-grubbing bankers in the wicked East. Douglas met their needs, and then some.

In Britain, Douglas was promising to take over the Bank of England in the name of the people. The evils of the current monetary system were the work of the socialists at the London School of Economics who were funded by the bankers. As well, Douglas advocated shutting down the "chatter box" at Westminster. The proper role of Parliament should be to appoint experts to run the economy. Douglas had all the right stuff to attract any Jew hater, red baiter, "non-partisan" politician, or fundamentalist Christian with an evangelical bent. You could buy it all or just use the bits that appealed to you.

The United Farmers decided to hire Douglas as their chief reconstruction adviser, but ultimately found his solutions too outrageous. He did, however, convince one man: William Aberhart – Bible Bill – a fifty-seven-year-old radio evangelist and would-be politician, and the Dean of the Prophetic Bible Institute. Bible Bill's solution was to give every Alberta resident twenty-five dollars. Douglas observed that Aberhart's knowledge of Social Credit theory was practically nil; but that didn't bother Aberhart or his followers in the Social Credit League.

Bible Bill told his people to tone down all that A-plus-B stuff as they headed into the 1935 provincial election. "You don't have to understand electricity to use it," he would say. "Facts, the REAL things," he told the electorate, "have only to be straightened up a little, rearranged, and poverty will cease to exist." He blew the United Farmers away and swept into power with fifty-seven of sixty-three seats.

In the federal election that followed all seventeen Alberta seats went Socred. Aberhart did some fiddling with financial institutions and interest rates, to the shock and horror of Major Douglas. Substantive legislation, however, was blocked by the lieutenant-governor, the courts, or the federal government; and Aberhart and Douglas parted ways. But Social Credit flourished in spirit if not in practice, and the party held power until 1971 when they were decimated by Peter Lougheed's Tories. In B.C., meanwhile, the movement simmered; it would take another fifteen years to come to a boil.

Wacky was not what you would call a family man – he would share that quality with his son Billy. Wacky's life was business and politics. And that took him away from home more and more over the years. The children and the house were left to May, whose schedule was built around his. Yet Wacky's presence overshadowed all else. When he was home, he would bounce out of bed every morning, bellow "It Couldn't Be Done", shave, and dress. He would eat, read the paper and listen to the radio all at the same time before heading to the store to prove that it could. After a quick supper he was usually off to a political function or service-club meeting. Weekends, he worked. Billy claims his earliest memories involved work – first the chores around the house and then, at age thirteen, work at his dad's hardware store every day after school and Saturdays.

Shortly after Wacky arrived in Kelowna he joined the local Board of Trade; he was vice-president for two years, then president for another two. He joined the Freemasons and a service club called the Gyros. He volunteered for the Canadian Red Cross. And every day he'd shoot the breeze

with his regular clutch of cronies over coffee. His involvement with the Tories started almost as soon as he took over
the hardware store: he became secretary-treasurer of the
Yale Conservative Association and vice-president of the
Kelowna and District Conservative Association.

The 1933 election was a watershed for B.C. politics: the
provincial Tories were trounced by Duff Pattullo's Liberals
and a new socialist party. Previously, B.C. had been a
two-party state, although there were certainly socialists
around and the province had a history of radical politics.
B.C.'s resource-based economy encouraged large militant
trade unions to do battle with mine operators, timber
barons, buccaneer businessmen, and absentee company
owners.

In 1933 the Regina Manifesto was signed into life, and
the Socialist Hordes found their voice in a coalition of
farmers, trade unionists, and socialists, in a newly minted
political force, the Co-operative Commonwealth Federation, the CCF. The B.C. election was the party's first testing
ground. Class warfare jumped into provincial politics and
the CCF, picking up almost a third of the popular vote and a
handful of seats, emerged as the official Opposition.

Wacky's first crack at a provincial nomination came in
what was South Okanagan in 1937. Despite years of service
to the constituency, his ambition, and his tireless efforts to
rebuild a broken Tory party, he was beaten by Tom Norris,
the nomination choice of the party's Vancouver establishment. Norris lost the election; the seat and the government
were taken by Pattullo's Liberals.

Pattullo used a style that both Wacky and Bill would
eventually adopt: fight the federal government with one
hand and the socialists with the other. The Tories beat out a
bickering, divided CCF by one seat and formed the Opposition, but Wacky was noticeably absent from the trenches.
He managed to rebuild his base in the Valley, took the 1941
nomination, and won his first provincial election. All the
kids helped. The Tories, however, dropped behind the CCF,
and the Liberals held only enough seats to form a minority
government.

Canada was well into the Second World War, and the debate in Victoria centred on forming a wartime government – a coalition of all three parties, for the good of the country. The Tories, under Pat Maitland, were guaranteed certain key portfolios by Pattullo's Liberals and jumped at the chance. The CCF, under Harold Winch, refused. They had been elected the official Opposition and they would remain the Opposition. None of this "non-partisan" talk for them. The Liberals and Tories went ahead with a coalition government that held power for the next decade.

At first Wacky was a jubilant backbencher enthralled with the "non-partisan" nature of the government. He was, he claimed, twice invited to join the coalition cabinet but refused – he still had a hardware business to build. But he soon became disgruntled with the old-line politicians and would, from time to time, vote with the CCF against the government. His fascination with the form of government soon subsided and was replaced by a growing frustration with his own party and by his ambition to influence and lead. He took his first shot at the provincial leadership of the Tories in 1946. No luck.

Bennett became even more of a maverick after Herbert Anscomb took over the party. Wacky ran as a Tory in a 1948 federal by-election in the riding of Yale and lost to the CCF candidate; but from the experience Wacky carried away two great lessons. First, he saw that the CCF had won because the free-enterprisers split their vote between the Liberals and the Tories. Second, he figured he had hurt his image by campaigning through this working-class riding in his flashy Packard sedan. In the future he would drive only "people's cars". This lesson would not be lost on Billy (although he did lust after that Packard once he got his driver's licence and developed an appetite for female company).

In 1950 Wacky went after Anscomb and the Tory leadership again, and again he lost, although his attacks on the degenerating coalition government increased. Finally Wacky rebelled on the issue of hospital-insurance-premium increases. On March 16, 1951, the Premium Amendment Act came up for debate. Wacky kicked things off with an hour-long harangue. He hammered the Liberals. He hammered the Tories. He hammered the Coalition. Then he crossed the floor to sit as an independent.

During the summer of 1951, Wacky hit the road once more, travelling across the country to see what party or government appealed to him. In Alberta he found that the Social Credit government had developed into a "non-partisan" system with a weak legislature dominated by the cabinet and a strong leader who tended to ignore his critics. It also had a certain Christian evangelism and a fiscal policy that emphasized balanced budgets and reduced debt. This was an appealing model for the man in search of a movement to lead.

While Social Credit was thriving in Alberta, it remained a fringe group in British Columbia. It was funded mostly by Alberta money, and its conventions had difficulty attracting enough people to elect an executive. During the 1945 provincial election a handful of Socred candidates, backed by British Israelites, monetary reformers, cranks, and Jew haters, picked up about 1.5 per cent of the popular vote. In 1948, the fringe split into the Social Credit Party and the Social Credit League. Both factions ran candidates in the 1949 election. Their total vote increased, but men who three years later would win an election and form a government were still drawing a mostly lunoid following.

That all changed as the Coalition crumbled and Wacky started meeting with the leaders of the tiny Social Credit League of B.C., looking for an opening. Wacky decided to test the strength of Social Credit – and the relative weakness of the Coalition – by running a Socred candidate in an Esquimalt by-election on October 1, 1951. He plucked a candidate out of nowhere and tossed in $10,000 of his own money. The Socred came second, behind the CCF but well ahead of the Coalition candidate.

Wacky had found a party that could win and a movement in search of a leader. But taking over that leadership provided one of the most bizarre yarns in B.C. political history.

Alberta's Premier Manning still had the funny idea that he ran the B.C. Socreds just because his party was bankrolling the operation, and he would occasionally summon errant B.C. Socreds to Alberta to chew them out. At the 1952 convention, the B.C. party outgrew the phone-booth stage. The convention attracted more than a thousand people. The meeting began with the singing of a hymn: "O God Our Help in Ages Past". Reporters were tossed out of the room, and the Alberta members started twisting arms to elect a campaign chairman from "outside of B.C." In the dying moments of the convention, when there was still no party leader, a motion was passed making it possible for the elected members of the party to choose their own leader.

In the election of 1952 Social Credit entered leaderless and emerged, thanks to the idiosyncrasies of the transferable ballot, as the party with the largest number of elected members. (The transferable ballot allows a voter to rank his choice of candidates. If no candidate achieves 50 per cent of the votes plus one, the candidate with the least number of votes is dropped, and the ballots are recounted, with second-choice votes applied, registered from the ballots where the dropped candidate was first choice. In a close three-way race where, for example, there are two free-enterprisers and a socialist running, this system favours a free-enterprise victory.) The CCF beat the Socreds in the popular vote but picked up fewer seats.

A quick meeting was held by the nineteen Socred MLAS, people who needed name tags to get around the small gathering and a road map to navigate the legislature. In that batch of teachers, preachers, auto mechanics, and up-country shopkeepers, only Wacky and the champion of coloured margarine for B.C., Tillie Rolston, had any experience in Victoria. Wacky was elected leader and, after considerable nail chewing by the lieutenant-governor, was called upon to form a government. Wacky's first cabinet toasted its success with Ovaltine.

Wacky took over the government with a vengeance. The first thing he did was announce a civil-service hiring freeze

and a plan to trim the public service. When he finally called
the legislature together, his budget was the first in provincial history actually to reduce government spending – an
act that wouldn't be duplicated for three decades. While
Billy, Anita, and R.J. peered over the wooden railings of the
visitors' gallery, soaking it all in, their father was on the
floor wielding power like a broadaxe. When the opposition
didn't like his legislation Wacky would refuse to adjourn
the legislature, forcing MLAs to talk all night long. Legislation by exhaustion; debate turned to gibberish. His con-
tempt for the legislature was palpable.

When he decided to put an end to his minority government, thinking the time was right for a majority, Wacky
introduced some purposefully provocative legislation on
education financing. The whole opposition force rose up
against him. Even members of his own caucus rebelled. It
was the first time in the fifty-three-year history of the
house that a government was defeated on the floor of the
legislature.

Wacky just grinned.

He was returned with a clear majority; the CCF was in
opposition and the old-line Liberals and Tories were in
tatters. Wacky crowed that B.C. was once again a two-party
state: the "non-partisan" Christians in government and the
Socialist Hordes threatening all things bright and beautiful
from the Opposition benches. Then he began a relentless
assault on trade-union power that would last through his
full twenty years as premier.

During the summer before Wacky's first government
met, B.C. was particularly beset by strikes. Wacky would
introduce legislation to reduce the possibility in the future.
He tossed out the old industrial conciliation and arbitration laws and brought in the new Labour Relations Act,
which gave his minister of labour wide discretionary
powers. During the summer of 1958, part of the privately
operated ferry system serving Vancouver Island was
struck, and the rest was about to be shut down. Bennett
invoked the Civil Defence Act and took over the Black Ball
Ferry Line. He would build his own ferry system rather

than be pushed around by the unions: "We won't let a few labour bosses or business bosses boss this government." The following day he told a Socred convention: "We won't hesitate to oppose labour leaders who use the labour movement for their own political CCF advancement."

When the legislature met in early 1959, government ministers howled against the unions and Jimmy Hoffa-style "gangsterism" in the B.C. labour movement. Their scare campaign was shrill if not convincing. The minister of public works claimed: "We are now witnessing perhaps in greater measure than ever before the misuse of power which labour leaders have acquired. . . . The original and legitimate intent of the union movement in some instances has been warped and twisted into a weapon in the hands of the wrong people." Then he muttered about "undesirable elements" and "unhealthy conditions". Two weeks later Wacky introduced his Trade Union Act. Paddy Sherman, a young legislative reporter at the time, wrote that the bill "imposed on labour by far the most restrictive curbs in Canada." Two years later Wacky introduced legislation to stop compulsory dues checkoffs should any union money go into political party coffers. Not surprisingly, this legislation coincided with the formation of the New Democratic Party, an alliance between the CCF and the Canadian Labour Congress.

Debt reduction, a carryover from his Depression days and a mainstay of Social Credit propaganda in Alberta, became a greater preoccupation with Bennett than thumping the trade-union movement. His first budget's measures to reduce government spending were never repeated by him, and his civil service grew and flourished despite his rhetoric. Yet he would say: "I do object most strongly to the principle . . . which mortgages our future, through excessive public borrowing, in return for a little less sacrifice and a little more comfort today." He reduced some small part of the debt – he was required to by statute – but then he embarked on the greatest bit of accounting acrobatics in the country. Most of the debt was simply transferred to Crown corporations or to school boards and hospital boards. And, as the province developed and Wacky exercised his considerable edifice complex, new roads were built, hydro projects proliferated, ferry fleets expanded, and towns sprouted with hospitals and schools. The per capita debt in B.C. exploded, but it was "indirect debt" not debt on the government's books.

In the summer of 1959, Wacky's baffling bookkeeping reached nirvana: he declared the province "debt free", and a massive celebration was prepared at his home on Okanagan Lake in Kelowna. At lunch his cabinet ministers were handed toy musical instruments and ordered to play. Wacky was given a fiddle to play during the evening's ceremonial bond burning. Through the warm afternoon some five hundred guests refreshed themselves with apple juice and tea until they were called upon to watch a swimming race. There were four boys in the race, representing the leaders of each political party. Amid great amounts of hooting and cheering, the boy representing Wacky was first across the finish line. Most people were probably too far into the apple juice to notice a thin underwater rope hauling Wacky's champion ahead of the pack.

Just after dusk, the guests assembled at the water's edge once again. The entire cabinet boarded a small launch and moved out to within fifteen feet of a barge anchored off shore. The barge was loaded with straw and a thin veneer of paid-up government bonds – $70 million worth – all held down by one-inch chicken wire. On the launch Wacky appeared with a bow and arrow. The arrow was set alight, and the Premier took careful aim. The arrow moved awkwardly across the chasm, bounced off the chicken wire, and fizzled into the lake. An RCMP officer stationed in a small boat behind the barge struck a match and torched the contents, and B.C. was purged of all fiscal evil.

Wacky would survive another thirteen years, charming British Columbians with his flamboyance and enraging them with his arrogance. He would maintain power by containing politics in a rigid two-party system and by what his biographer, David Mitchell, calls his "paranoid style", a regular dose of red baiting. In the end, disillusionment on the right and a mild Tory revival would do him in as much as anything else. At the final big Socred rally of the 1972 election campaign, when Wacky could smell defeat, there was a hint of desperation in his voice as he gave his well-worn rhetoric one more try: "I want to tell you tonight, that the Socialist Hordes are at the gates of British Columbia." He lost the election but passed on to British Columbia and to his son Billy an indelible style.

2
BILLY

Billy Bennett grew from an infant to a young child in one of the most magnificent houses in the Okanagan Valley, a two-story stone and wood mansion on seven acres of lawns and orchards with a small stream; it was picked up from the mortgage company after the previous owner went under in the Depression and died penniless. Except when the cotton-wood poplars were shedding or the orchards were in blossom and his hay fever forced him into the house, Billy had all the wonders of nature to explore in the safety of a remote, small town. He was surrounded and nurtured by totally dedicated women: his mother, his sister, Anita, and Winnie Earle, a young woman who came to the Bennett home as a temporary housekeeper and never left. They ensured that he lacked for nothing and that he was disciplined when he terrorized the neighbourhood or plunged into the irrigation ditches. When Anita tired of chasing him around she tied him to the cherry tree in the yard. All three women watched him as he did his chores, practised his trumpet, or played in the orchard at the back of the house. To Billy the Depression was little more than a regular procession of panhandlers who would turn up at the back door and, at his father's insistence, be shown the woodpile and an axe before they were offered a plate of food. Billy Bennett wanted for no material thing.

From as far back as Bill Bennett can remember there were politics and money. "We were raised in the political environment – the whole conversation around the family was one enjoyable argument," he recalls. His mother "conned" Wacky into taking Billy on a train trip to his first political convention, the Progressive Conservative national convention in Ottawa. He was six years old, and his trip was a brief respite from the heavy pollen that filled the Okanagan air. "That's where I got a lesson on how to get ahead in life. I think I knew these people [on the train] were special, with their talk and their forcefulness and the way they carried themselves. I used to hang around the club car, probably bored, while my father was talking with all these people, and I'd be flipping a quarter from the dollar I'd saved from my ten-cent-a-week allowance. This time the quarter flipped into the spittoon. Now, I can't remember who it was – he was a leading politician, perhaps even a premier – but when I started to cry, he reached into the spittoon, fished the quarter out, dried it off, and then gave me another quarter along with it. I spent the rest of the trip trying to flip quarters into the spittoon."

Money became a compulsion. When he wasn't flipping quarters he was saving nickels at Don Terry's ice-cream parlour in Kelowna. Don sold ice-cream sodas. Billy figured that he and his buddies could save a nickel apiece by bringing in their own brick of ice cream, ordering soft drinks, and making up their own soda floats.

He was always the most ambitious of Wacky's three kids. And his ambition, which a friend remembers as his "killer instinct", first surfaced on the basketball court. That this pint-sized kid made the team at all was testimony to his single-mindedness. His mother remembers that "basketball was his big thing. He wanted to be six feet and he didn't quite get that tall."

What really caught young Billy's fancy in high school, though, were the girls. Pretty girls. And there were lots of them. His wife, Audrey, remembers that Billy didn't take any notice of her at all until she entered in the "Lady of the Lake" beauty pageant. Billy could charm the girls' socks off cruising the valley in Wacky's Packard. One buddy discovered that even this pastime had a compulsive side when Billy took him up to his bedroom, pulled open a dresser drawer, and showed him an earring collection. There were "about seventeen" in all. Trophies.

Work for young Billy seemed, at first, less a passion than a duty. His mother set the schedule for all three kids in their daily chores: they dusted the stairs, brought in wood for the stove, emptied the ashes, and took out the garbage. By the time Billy reached his teens he was working in his dad's store. It was what you did if you were Wacky's kid. And you also bought your own clothes with money you made.

Billy bailed out of an uninspired high-school career with the minimum requirement for graduation. He was pleased that he didn't go any further. He said that going to university and picking up a law degree would serve only to "complicate my mind" with legalese. But even before his formal education petered out, he was teamed up with his brother, R.J., trying to make money on anything that moved. When their shot at a market garden failed, they converted the tractor into a portable sawmill and bucked firewood. When he left school, Bill went into hardware and furniture with R.J. They had their own stores as well as Wacky's chain. Once Kelowna was linked with the outside world by a bridge across the lake and a new Hope-Princeton highway, the Bennett boys were in the right place at the right time for a real-estate boom; they bought and built their way right up the valley and clear to Kamloops. The tireless days and nights that Wacky's lads spent hauling, sawing, buying, and selling are legend to this day in the Okanagan Valley. Nothing was allowed to stand in Bill's acquisitive path, not even the dream home an architect friend designed for Audrey and him when they were newlyweds. The house was liquidated to provide capital for a motel operation Bill picked up; he and Audrey moved into the owner's apartment. Bill would recall that "if anything came out of our upbringing it was the self-discipline we learned." And the self-discipline that he first applied to making money he later applied to running the province.

His relations with his father were more formal and formidable than those he enjoyed with the household of doting women. Bill was nine years old in 1941 when his dad first became the member from South Okanagan and started his annual three-month sojourn in Victoria as a young Tory MLA. As an adult Bill would most often refer to his father as "the former premier" or "the former member from South Okanagan". Wacky handed out a licking to young Billy exactly six times in his life, and Bill remembered each of those times distinctly long after his father died. "When he hit you, you didn't forget it." Bill was twenty when his father became premier. Bill and R.J. were at work in one of their father's five stores when the phone call came from Victoria. Wacky told them he would have to spend more of his time away from home. No time for the business. I want you boys to be "in complete control", he said. He wouldn't be ordering so much as another nail; but he might drop by the office to run a gimlet eye over the ledgers now and then. The boys were in control, but they weren't partners, in anything. Wacky left the stores to his wife and, after her death, to his grandchildren.

Bill Bennett would enter adulthood a driven man. Driven to win; driven to outrun his father's shadow. The "killer instinct" of his basketball days stayed with him. His coarse confrontational style in sports, particularly in tennis – the major social activity in his life – became a metaphor for his political style. Underestimate the man at your peril. Jim Matkin, then a young deputy minister, did once – on a tennis court.

Look at that game from Matkin's point of view. Here comes Bennett, with his awkward, flat-footed, bowlegged walk. Although his body is trim, even sinewy – the man is fanatically fit – it looks stiff, rather than athletic. He hauls out the biggest racket Matkin has ever seen.

The Game begins. Bennett does not exhibit much finesse, but he is forceful, intimidating, relentless. He ruggedly works Matkin from one side of the court to the other. Then a drop shot. What he lacks in style he makes up for in strategy, wearing Matkin down, looking for a weak spot and playing to it. Because of his huge racket and his tenacity, Bennett can return almost any shot.

Bennett's serve is not particularly powerful, but it has a lot of junk on it. When you figure you've got the junk sorted out, he changes it. Matkin starts out playing easy, figuring he is the better player. Soon he starts playing hard, but he is soundly whipped. He feels humiliated, stupid. Matkin decides to stick to friendly games of doubles in the future. Bill Bennett is a sore winner. Bennett's deputy minister, Norman Spector, limits his encounters to more cerebral matters. When asked about Bennett's game, Pat McGeer, the tennis ace in the Socred cabinet, takes on one of those spread-eagle grins of a man with something to hide. All he will say is that the Premier plays a "very aggressive" game. For McGeer, the problem isn't losing to Bennett, it is winning. The cold shoulder would freeze a lake in August.

The public Bill Bennett is very different from the private man his friends and advisers describe. They say he's keenly interested in the minutiae of political history and intrigue. With them, they say, he is witty and glib. But in public there is only a clattering, mechanical laugh and a nervous tick: it starts with a winking right eye; then he presses his tongue hard into the side of his mouth and pushes it around, as a blue glow spreads over his jowls, highlighting his perpetual five o'clock shadow. His public speech lacks the eloquence his sister remembers from his youth. He is a bundle of run-on sentences, curious summations, inexplicable digressions, and mangled metaphors. In the aftermath of a clutch of Socred scandals, Bill's comment was: "This is a party that speaks its mind straight from the shoulder."

In public, he is decidedly boring. The word "intellect" is not apropos. His sister, though, says he's no dummy. She says he read the complete works of Dickens before he entered high school. But Little Nell and Tiny Tim have since been drowned in a sea of ink from government documents.

Yet, when the man heads east across the mountains, his public persona appears transformed. A *Globe and Mail* editorial described Bill Bennett while he was chairing the meetings of the premiers' constitutional battle with Pierre Trudeau. The editorial stunned British Columbians, who have seen Bill duck, bob, weave, and sputter incoherently. "He is," the *Globe* observed, "an intelligent man, retiring, but good with words . . . . He is inventive. He is conciliatory." Could *Globe* publisher A. Roy Megarry have been pumping up Bennett in his attempt to derail the Trudeau patriation effort?

"A man's man." That's what Jimmy Pattison calls Bill Bennett. "He's a businessman's businessman. . . . The positive side about Bill Bennett is that he really cares about money." Jimmy has worked for Bennett since 1981, first as head of Expo 86 and then as head of Expo and B.C. Place. Pattison doesn't charge Bennett a nickel for his time. Bill Bennett is "no B.S. No baloney. You know . . . a lot of people in government talk in long sentences and big paragraphs and don't say anything. Bennett talks straight English."

Bennett is a loner. His few friends are all in Kelowna. And they do not spend a lot of time talking about B.C. politics. Bill Bennett is no Brian Mulroney or John Turner; he has no countrywide network of friends and advisers that go back to his school days. Bennett does not socialize with members of his cabinet or with people doing business with government. You could count his political confidants on the fingers of one tightly clenched fist. Only two cabinet ministers are within hailing distance of the man: Bob McClelland, an ex-trucker from Alberta, was the Minister of Labour responsible for unloading the human rights workers and dismantling union rights in British Columbia in 1983 and 1984. Don Phillips is Minister of Industry, Trade and Commerce and Bennett's new magnet for foreign investment. Phillips is a leather-lunged, silver-tongued orator from the big-sky country of the South Peace, an immigrant from the Maritimes, a former used-car dealer.

Cheery little trumpet-playing Billy can take on a morose, guarded quality. His sister Anita remarks: "I don't think Bill has as many of the joys of spring in his life as Father had." Even more than his father, he would carefully, almost compulsively, compartmentalize his life. His family plays virtually no role in his public world. Even when he comes home to Kelowna, his sanctuary, he is obsessed by his work; his wife, Audrey, and their four boys have "learned the hard way" not to get in his road. "We feel very, very sorry for him," Audrey confides, "and we wish there was some way we could help him. But there isn't. We just have to sit and watch. There's not much you can do about it."

Nor was Wacky at his son's elbow to direct and advise. Lots rubbed off the old man, but it came almost in spite of their relationship. In the spring of 1978, Bill Bennett had been premier for two and a half years. Wacky Bennett was sitting in the living room of his waterfront apartment in Oak Bay, and May was off in the kitchen, when the telephone rang. It was Jean Chrétien, the federal Minister of Finance. It was not uncommon for the two men to talk on the phone, to discuss Chrétien's upcoming budget, to talk about business and finance. Chrétien had known Wacky for years and dealt with him as premier. The old man was lonely. Chrétien wanted to cheer him up. Even before Bill's election victory, Wacky had been cut off, considered an albatross; he was a man who did not feel welcome in his son's new hardware store. He needed an ear for his ideas, and he had to get it from a federal Liberal.

Wacky's biographer, David Mitchell, has summed up this odd father-son relationship: "Bill Bennett ran from his father, not to him. Every son has to fight to free himself from his father, but with Bill Bennett that struggle sometimes seemed the equivalent of a kind of psychic patricide." When Wacky died on the evening of February 23, 1979, overcome by old age and the complications that follow a stroke, at his side, Mitchell carefully notes, were "his dedicated wife, daughter Anita, and eldest son, R.J." No Bill.

Making it on his own was Bill's obsession; yet his father's helping hand was everywhere once Bill decided to take over the seat vacated by "the former member from South Okanagan". Even Wacky's decision to resign his seat before the Socred leadership convention was a shrewd way of tilting the race in his son's favour. The old man called in a lifetime of political debts from the nominating meeting; he stacked the Socred leadership convention with hand-picked Bennett supporters who were bused to the convention from Vancouver Island and the B.C. interior while the Bennett machine picked up most or all of their costs for transportation, accommodation, and meals.

With the leadership won, while Bill was down in Victoria generally being abused by Dave Barrett and the first socialist government in the history of the province, Wacky worked at rebuilding the party and beating the NDP in the countryside. He took the Socred research staff – two of his former cabinet ministers, Dan Campbell and Grace McCarthy – and toured the province in his "freedom bus", spreading propaganda about Barrett plundering the provincial piggy bank and the "foreign socialist" ideology that held B.C. in its grip. At mass rallies Wacky introduced Gracie as "British Columbia's number one freedom fighter". Campbell was "Dangerous Dan", a threat to the Socialist Hordes.

Gracie went on a Socred membership-card selling spree that would put to shame the Vegematic salesmen at the Pacific National Exhibition. Yessiree folks, it's a fight for freedom! Step right up and buy your Social Credit membership. Just one thin five-dollar bill will buy you four freedom-filled years. In 1974 alone she sold 32,000 memberships. By the time the 1975 election rolled around there were 75,000 card-carrying Socreds jumping up and down in the largest political crusade in Canadian history. Of course, the paltry membership fee wouldn't pay to update the membership mailing lists, but corporate money was just a phone call away.

Businessmen were handing over bundles of cash to any and all groups that looked as if they could take on the Hordes and beat them back. The most serious free-enterprise threat to take over from a limping, bleeding Socred Opposition was the Majority Movement. When Wacky got wind of it, he hauled one of its contributors over to Gracie's house in chic Shaughnessy and went up one side of him and down the other. The businessman asked the Majority Movement for his money back, and others soon followed. One night in early 1974, Wacky got an urgent phone call from Bill asking him to phone Robert Bonner, once Wacky's most trusted cabinet minister and attorney general, now head man at MacMillan Bloedel. Bonner was being wooed by the Majority Movement to take on the leadership. Within two days Wacky turned him around by arguing, somewhat prematurely, that Social Credit was still a political force that could win; Bonner was eventually brought into the fold to head up B.C. Hydro.

When the election writ was dropped, however, Wacky was put on ice for good. Shortly after Bill won the party leadership in November 1973, a group of well-heeled B.C. businessmen, most of them connected with the mining community, threw some money in a pot and phoned Martin Goldfarb in Toronto. Goldfarb, Canada's best-known political pollster, whose star client was the Liberal Party of Canada, had a number of private-sector clients in B.C. The mining industry was practically deranged because of the tax legislation on mineral royalties brought down by the NDP government. The mining industrialists were determined to unload the legislation as fast as they could and wanted Goldfarb to lend Bill Bennett a hand.

The interests backing the Goldfarb project included Bethlehem Copper, Rio Algom, and Cominco. Prominent among the group who contacted Goldfarb were Pat Reynolds, the head of Bethlehem Copper, Senator John Nichol, an old friend of Goldfarb's through his Liberal Party connections, and Austin Taylor, Jr., head boy at the Vancouver offices of McLeod Young Weir. Taylor, all 325 pounds and six foot six inches of him, was Bill Bennett's very first bagman. (He moved on to run McLeod's head office in Toronto and to manage the B.C. government's forays into the financial markets of the world.) The proposition put to

Goldfarb was: would he figure out a way to whip Dave Barrett? Goldfarb hopped a plane and flew out to the coast.

Goldfarb prepared two studies on Barrett's British Columbia and began to map out a strategy for the committee putting up the bucks. After his second study, Goldfarb was called to make a presentation and meet Bill Bennett in Austin Taylor's living room in Vancouver. Bennett arrived with two others: Dangerous Dan Campbell, who was teaching Bennett the finer points of political manoeuvring and handing him a safety razor and a box of No. 4 powder whenever he came in range of a TV camera; and Bennett's new public-relations adviser, David Brown, an Englishman who had toiled for fourteen years at Baker Lovick, the ad agency that had handled the old Socred government's account and did work for – you guessed it – the mining industry.

There was a bit of bravado, especially from Bennett and Campbell. Goldfarb remembers that in those days Bennett was still a novice. He couldn't deliver a speech. He was trading on his father's reputation and regurgitating a lot of business-baron rhetoric. Bennett said he had a lot of his own good research: Goldfarb asked to see it. Bennett said, "I've knocked on five thousand doors in the last few months and have a hell of a staff." Goldfarb said, "With all due respect, that's bullshit. Stop playing games with us. If you want us to get involved professionally, we'll get involved. If you don't, fine, I'll withdraw."

At this point, Taylor inserted his considerable bulk into the debate and said he wanted Goldfarb in; and he was in. Bill Bennett and the Socreds hired their first pollster. Taylor asked for a budget and a strategy that would take them into the 1975 election and help Bill deal with the issues. But first there was the problem of Bill Bennett's confrontationist personality. Goldfarb asked him to tone it down.

The tactical problem facing Bennett was how to undermine the Liberal and Conservative vote, form the coalition, and get Pat McGeer and the Liberals on side. The Socreds knew that the NDP had a solid 40 per cent core vote; this meant they had to reduce the Liberal and Tory vote to less than 15 per cent so that the Socreds could have a shot at winning.

The Majority Movement had run out of steam, to a large extent as a result of the efforts of Wacky Bennett. Tory MLA Hugh Curtis and provincial Tory party president Peter Hyndman, along with Surrey mayor and former Liberal Bill Vander Zalm, were already pitching their tents in the Socred camp.

Spring 1975 found Liberal MLA Pat McGeer drifting around Ottawa talking to any federal Liberal he could lay his lips on, testing the waters on a planned defection by him, Allan Williams, and Garde Gardom to Bill Bennett's Socreds, a move that would help deep-six the provincial Liberals until well into the 1980s. Ironically, he was there with the assistance of the then premier, Dave Barrett, who had instituted the practice of bringing along opposition members when he attended federal-provincial conferences. The practice did not continue under Bill Bennett.

Goldfarb became a quiet, unobtrusive resource, developing strategy and doing research. He even tested the advertising the Socreds used heading into the 1975 election. And while Barrett was falling all over himself on the way to the polls, Goldfarb turned up one area that was giving Barrett particular problems: education.

Barrett's problem was remarkably similar to the pickle Bill Bennett was also to find himself in. The government was seen as meddling in the affairs of the local school boards; teachers felt threatened. Old values were being challenged; parents were outraged. Bill Bennett's 1975 education platform read like a 1985 speech by the NDP education critic. Bennett actually said: "The minister of education seems determined to gain control of all educational facilities within our province . . . at the expense of local school boards. This move to central control means confusion and frustration for local board members . . . and, more important, it means that educational policies are being developed with no real consideration for the needs and wishes of local areas. We would return authority to local school boards ... we would also return dignity and responsibility to individual classroom teachers – trained professionals who deserve more authority in setting educational objectives for their pupils."

The Socred team was in place: David Brown handled the publicity; Dan Campbell kept Bill's nose powdered; Bill Bennett wooed the Liberals and the Tories; Austin Taylor raised the cash; Marty Goldfarb crunched the numbers and test marketed the slogans. The old party hands were there with just a dash of modernity, like country boys with credit cards. And Dave Barrett fulfilled their fondest desires by screwing up all the way.

A style of politics was developing. What Bill Bennett had learned at his father's knee was becoming his most potent weapon: the politics of polarization that Wacky Bennett had used to encourage the development of a rigid two-party system.

It would take some time, but Bill Bennett modernized and refined his father's technique. He would never be a conciliator on the stump – that would have been certain political death. Goldfarb discovered that "The mass group in B.C. is at the polarity, which is different than other parts of Canada. The middle is very shallow. The trick for Bennett is to keep it that way ... as long as there are extremes, as long as the political spectrum in B.C. is polarized, the NDP can't get elected. As soon as it becomes unpolarized, the NDP will get elected." The strategy worked. The coalition on the right formed and held like cement. The socialists were sunk.

Bill Bennett's first two terms in government were stumbling affairs. Goldfarb's talents were mostly used for planning elections. At other times Bill would drift about relying mostly on his own political instincts. The party was virtually the same disorganized, antiquated bit of machinery Wacky had left behind. No real change took place until the nearly disastrous election of 1979 when Bill was desperate for a victory and called on his old friend Hugh Harris.

Hugh Harris was a rare creature in Bennett's life. This

amiable, bearded, discreetly tattooed pipe smoker bridged
the chasm that separates Bennett's few friends from his
even fewer political advisers. Harris was an east-end Vancouver kid who turned up hustling real estate in Kelowna in
the early 1970s. Following the 1972 election, the Social
Credit party lay in ruins. Wacky Bennett had told his con-
stituents he was stepping down. Twenty-five Kelowna
businessmen gathered at one of their regular watering holes
to decide whom they would back in the by-election, and
then in the inevitable general election, to replace Wacky.
They had two choices: Bill Bennett, whose highest elected
public offices to date were president of the Kelowna Chamber of Commerce and grade 9 student-council rep; and the
new leader of the B.C. Tories, a young lawyer and new-
comer to Kelowna society named Darril Warren. The vote
was twenty-two to three in Warren's favour. When Bill
heard about the decision he went on an arm-twisting mission against his old high-school buddies. Warren was left to
wither and die. In the by-election, the boys were behind
Bill, and his friend Hugh Harris became his campaign manager. Hugh's wife, Meldy, took over as president of the
local Socred organization.

Seven years later, Hugh would again be summoned from
flogging Okanagan Valley property to rescue the 1979 campaign. It's hard to determine what specifically pulled Bennett through, but it was probably his first public act of
privatization: BCRIC, the British Columbia Resources Investment Corporation. Bennett took the bundle of resource-based companies and gas-drilling leases that the
NDP government had scooped up for about $40 million and
turned them over to the private sector when they were
worth more than ten times their purchase value. Everybody
in the province whose breath could fog a mirror was given
five free BCRIC shares. Many were convinced to cash in their
life savings on shares at six bucks a crack. People's
capitalism.

Pollster Marty Goldfarb was back writing the strategy for
Bill, for the first time since the 1975 election. Dave Brown
was putting together the ad campaign that Goldfarb would

test market. Until Hugh Harris got the call, Dangerous Dan Campbell was in over-all charge of the operation.

From the few loose facts assembled from a very loose campaign a picture emerges of Dangerous Dan wandering about the B.C. countryside with his pudgy little hand wrapped around $60,000 in petty cash raised by Austin Taylor, Jr. Dan was dishing out thousand-dollar bills to pay for various and sundry. No receipts, thank you very much – that would just mean more paper to worry about. The Social Credit research department had prepared a campaign strategy independently of Goldfarb, packaged on cassette tapes and mailed out to election headquarters around the province. High-tech dirty tricks. The Lettergate scandal. The strategy included a variety of creative deceptions – none of which, the RCMP later concluded, was illegal: writing phony letters to the editor in praise of the Socreds, signed with fictitious names that resembled listings in the phone book; writing letters attacking the NDP signed with names of prominent New Democrats; jamming the lines of radio phone-in shows, saying things like: "I voted NDP last time but those suckers aren't getting my vote this time. I'm voting Social Credit." Meanwhile, Bill Bennett's road show was such a disaster he was reported to be literally flying in circles over ridings he didn't stand a chance of winning.

Enter Hugh Harris, armed with bailing wire and chewing gum.

After he won the election, Bennett moved to take over a party apparatus that was in chaos. Dan Campbell was put on ice in Victoria. He would have been shipped off to his final reward at B.C. House in London, but news of those free-flowing thousand-dollar bills had surfaced. He was, instead, kicked away from the trough and exiled to his summer home on Cortes Island. To a chorus of yowls from the old-line Socreds, Hugh Harris was made the first permanent executive director of the party. Meldy resigned as president of Bill Bennett's local organization and packed up the kids to join Hugh in Vancouver and Socred headquarters.

Hugh Harris had no sooner settled in than he began to travel. During the next two years he managed to take in every major election in North America. Where he could, he wandered into campaign headquarters and introduced himself; then he watched and listened or asked questions. He met Democratic strategists and Republican pollsters, Liberal propagandists and Tory backroom boys. Hugh was looking for talent and technique. The advantage the NDP had built up over the years – the ability to draw on a nation-wide talent pool – was about to be lost.

The test came in the May 1981 Kamloops by-election. Even though the riding had been won by the Socreds in 1979, and the economy was booming right along, Bill Bennett was beleaguered by the dirty-tricks election scandals left over from 1979. And there is nothing like a by-election to send a message to the government.

Harris moved up from the lower mainland and flooded the riding with volunteer organizers from all over the province. The candidate, Claude Richmond, had grown up in the riding and was a popular local politician and radio personality. When Harris set up his phone banks and canvassing schedules, he used techniques perfected by the NDP. Money was no object.

The NDP went into the campaign half-asleep. Their senior campaign strategist, Yvonne Cocke, figured she could run the operation from the coast, since the NDP was a full ten points ahead of the Socreds in Kamloops. Dave Barrett was out of the country for much of the campaign, including the crucial days just before the vote. The NDP campaign chairman figured that, yawn, nothing could beat the NDP machine. He ignored the fact that his candidate, a long-time local alderman, was a new boy. The ink was still wet on his NDP membership card, and he had won the nomination after a nasty three-way race that left a lot of hard-liners sitting at home on their hands for the rest of the campaign.

The Socreds pulled off a dazzling squeaker: they took the riding by eight hundred votes. While they boogied long into the night, a power failure plunged a sombre NDP wake into darkness. Anyone who doubted Harris before was now on side. He was well on his way to revolutionizing the Social Credit Party.

There was one thing, though, that Hugh Harris would not change: Bill Bennett's campaign style. If anything, more advantage would be taken of Bill's natural and inherited instincts to polarize and confront. Bill Bennett, the millionaire hardware merchant from the small town, the man's man, the loner, the kid constantly running from his father's shadow would emerge as a tough guy controlling a powerful new machine. He would become a man who, in Marty Goldfarb's words, "understands the base, crass motivations of the street, and he plays to them."

3

THE PARTY

An hour and a half into the party, Peter Brown has his arms around an anatomically correct, nude, female blow-up doll. This Socred bagman and head of the Expo 86 finance committee has recently been rewarded for his services with an appointment to the board of governors of the University of British Columbia, which he dropped out of almost two decades earlier. Brown is radiating beams of devilish joy on the landing of the circular staircase in Jake Kerr's spacious and otherwise tastefully appointed foyer. Jake Kerr is, among other things, head of a lumber wholesaling outfit called Lignum Sales; he is also on the boards of B.C. Rail and the Bank of British Columbia. The party is to celebrate Jake's fortieth birthday. It's September 1984, in the lull between yachting off the coast and skiing at Whistler.

Jake's seventy or so guests are Peter Newman's Acquisitors on the fringe of Canadian civilization. They are bright and bare knuckled. The Nouveau Socreds. The party, cut from the sombre conservative cloth of small-town shopkeepers and small-time car dealers, sports a new image: designer jeans, pastel Lacoste shirts, Gucci loafers. The centre shifts to the city; the party goes high-tech. Conspicuous consumption succeeds pennypinching.

These people are the heirs to a political coalition that has been part of B.C. history since the two old-line parties began to conspire against the CCF in the 1930s. They rededicated themselves to that task when the NDP took over in

Victoria in 1972. Now they regularly dip into their pig-
gybanks for the cause and occasionally roll up their sleeves
in the back rooms during election campaigns. And unlike
their country cousins, Bill Bennett and his buddies from
Kelowna, these hustlers and hedonists hold power and
party together.

To this crowd Brown is known as "Petesy", a monicker
that has stuck since his Zeta Psi fraternity days. Standing on
the landing next to Petesy and his inflatable doll is Jack
Poole, head of Daon Development Corporation and a regular at any gathering of this branch of Shaughnessy high-
rollers. Below, in the vestibule and living room, Edgar Kaiser, Jr., and Judy, his new wife – his third – are chatting with
Paul Manning. Paul was in Zeta Psi just a few years behind
Petesy; now he is between engagements. Most recently
Paul backed away from the Socred trough and his job at B.C.
Place, where Edgar sits on the board, to try once again
(without success) to win as a federal Liberal candidate. Paul
moves off to pick up a handful of garlic-salt-coated pea-
nuts, and Edgar has a word with Cindy Grauer. Cindy is
exhausted from her work for the Liberals in the federal
campaign. She is planning to take a month away. Not sure
what she'll do when she gets back. Edgar says: "Give me a
call." (Within days of this party Jake Kerr and his board at
the Bank of B.C. will make public the decision to hire Edgar
Kaiser as the bank's saviour and president. Edgar will then
hire Paul Manning as the bank's chief flak, Vice-president
of Corporate Communications. When Cindy returns from
her holiday and contacts Edgar, he will hire her as his
executive assistant.)

Paul and Cindy are not the lone Liberals at the party.
David Mindell is also munching and mingling. David,
whose money comes in part from hustling Osaga sneakers,
was John Turner's campaign organizer in Vancouver
Quadra earlier in the month. He is just walking past Harvey
Southam and his charming wife, Pia Shandel. Harvey's
money is a homegrown blend of the MacMillan forestry
fortunes on his mother's side and newspapers on his father's side. He is editor of the glossy Vancouver business

magazine *Equity*, and he frequently commissions profiles of the people in this room.

Nelson Skalbania and his wife, Eleni, look somewhat wilted from their financial difficulties, but they wouldn't miss a party. You all must know Malory Smith and his wife. Mal is still president of McGavin Foods Ltd. and still recalls his sudden departure as chairman of the Crown-owned B.C. Systems Corporation. Bill Bennett was not amused when Smith's board handed out juicy bonuses to the senior staff right in the middle of the government's restraint campaign.

Never mind, the entertainment is about to begin. Petesy frees one hand from the rubber lady and picks up a microphone, which is connected to the stereo system. He calls everyone around and invites Jake Kerr, the birthday boy, to come up the stairs for the presentation of gifts. Petesy hands Jake the blow-up. Then it's time for Jack Poole's offering. A raunchy bar tune is struck up on the stereo, and from the top of the stairway descends a dazzling vision of uncertain gender and overwhelming bulk. The small crowd seems torn between embarrassed tittering and full belly-laughs. It is a woman, well over six feet tall and weighing close to five hundred pounds. There is a feather boa around her neck. Her body is sheathed in floor-length red satin suspended by the most tenuous of spaghetti straps. Her face is caked with makeup, and her eyes have enough blue goop on them to last a string of drag queens for a week. This is Big Fanny Anny, a discovery of the late Joe Philliponi and his Penthouse strip-show emporium. When she reaches the landing, Jake props one elbow up on Big Fanny's bosom and mutters a few words. Anny then bumps down the stairs. First one spaghetti strap is shaken off a shoulder, then the other. The top of the gown falls forward. There is a momentary hush as she reveals two enormous breasts with nipples the size of plungers.

One couple who were invited to Kerr's soiree but sent their regrets were the Patrick Kinsellas. Patrick was temporarily back in Ontario preparing for the provincial Tory leadership race. Kinsella is the bit of big-city glitter who brought designer politics to the Nouveau Socred party. He was part of the Harris-instigated nationwide recruiting drive that went into high gear immediately following the stunning spring 1981 Kamloops by-election victory. By summer 1981, Hugh Harris was buying up the talent.

Imagine the kind of Okanagan Valley July scorcher that is bearable only if there is a breeze. On the hillsides the sun glints off the long, arching streams of water sucked up out of the deep cool lakes and spitting out of massive sprinklers. Beyond the reach of the water there is only browning coarse grass, tumbleweed, and cactus. Within the sprinklers' embrace there are thousands of acres of tomatoes, apples, pears, apricots, and grapes swelling in the heat to full size and ripeness.

Cutting along Okanagan Lake from Westbank, a small power boat approaches the west shore and a dock in front of a cottage at Fintry. Bill Bennett is standing at the wheel, stripped to the waist and tanned. Audrey is at his side. The cottage belongs to Hugh Harris. Among the buzzing, drinking, pleasant crowd assembled to meet the Premier is Jerry Lampert, a genial young Tory from Ontario. Hugh Harris plans to lure him to the coast.

Lampert and Harris first met in Toronto during Bill Davis's 1981 provincial election campaign – they just happened to be on the same plane heading up to Ottawa. Hugh and Jerry laughed and scratched about politics, organizing, and British Columbia. They parted with the political equivalent of "Let's do lunch." As eastern-Ontario organizer of Bill Davis's Big Blue Machine, Lampert was based in Ottawa. It was the latest of a long list of assignments he'd had as a political operative for the Tories. Lampert was a Tory activist as far back as his student days at Carleton in the late 1960s. He was president of the student society, when students were noisily making their demands known on campuses all across Canada. Young Tories like Lampert were in favour of the Committee for an Independent Canada and legalizing marijuana.

Lampert's soulmate, another young Tory and the president of the student society at the University of Ottawa, was Hugh Segal, who would become resident wit of Davis's Big Blue Machine. After Lampert graduated he worked in his dad's plumbing business and helped Hugh Segal with his political ambitions. Their close friendship began when they worked together on Segal's two unsuccessful candidacies for the federal parliament in Ottawa ridings in '72 and '74. In November 1974 Jerry Lampert got a phone call from John Laschinger, the national director of the Tory party. (A decade later, Lampert would have Laschinger's job.) Laschinger wanted Lampert to be part of the team organizing the leadership campaign that would replace Robert Stanfield with Joe Clark. That done, Clark hired Lampert as his administrative assistant, a job Lampert held until October 1977, shortly after the Ontario election in which Bill Davis was returned for the second time with a minority government. When Davis bumped Patrick Kinsella, his western-Ontario organizer, up to party executive director, Kinsella immediately got Jerry Lampert to handle eastern Ontario. That was the job Lampert held when he first met Harris.

Hugh Harris invited Lampert back out to the coast in May 1981 to put together a B.C. machine like the ones he had helped develop in Ontario and federally. Lampert had just been passed over for the job as executive director of the Ontario PC party. It was accept Harris's offer or go back to work for Joe Clark. No contest. Lampert's wife, a federal civil servant, put in for a Vancouver transfer. The chat with Bennett at Harris's cottage cinched the deal, and Lampert was on the coast before they were picking the pears in Bill Bennett's orchard.

As soon as Lampert came on board he hired three organizers, including the Tories' western-Canadian organizer, Dave Tkachuk from Saskatchewan. (Tkachuk has since returned home to work as Grant Devine's principal secretary.) Harris and Lampert also picked up Bruce Lane, the guy who organized campaign tours for Bill Davis and Joe Clark.

While Harris was wooing Lampert he was also after Patrick Kinsella. The idea was to put Lampert in party headquarters and Kinsella in Bill Bennett's office. They would clear out all the aging retainers, including Bill's Kelowna boyhood chum Tony Tozer, and then get a handle on the operation. Kinsella was bored with prospects in Ontario. Besides, his marriage was over, and the coast offered a loose, lush lifestyle that he thought he would find pleasant. And the prospect of operating Bill Bennett's political laboratory on this fertile frontier was intriguing.

Kinsella once called himself "the best political hack in the country". In Ontario he developed an appetite for dirty tricks. During a 1980 provincial by-election in Carleton, Jerry Lampert ran the local operation, and Kinsella played provincial quarterback. A *Globe and Mail* editorial observed that the Tories "used the sort of campaign literature which gives campaigns a bad name and which disgraces everyone concerned. . . ."

While he was still working full-time as an insurance salesman in his home town of Woodstock, south-west of London, Ontario, Kinsella had volunteered for Tory duty in the 1971 provincial campaign for a candidate with the unlikely name of Harry Parrott. By the mid 1970s Kinsella was a cog in the Big Blue Machine, and by 1977 he was well schooled in conservative political strategy: "We as Conservatives have a working relationship with the Republican Party in the United States," he points out. "And that allowed me to go to campaign schools, candidate colleges and so on, that the Republican Party puts on on a regular basis. And frankly I stole all their ideas."

Those ideas would be put to the test in British Columbia after October 1981, when Patrick Kinsella assumed his post as deputy minister to the premier. Kinsella took one look at his tatty government-issue decor and ordered $15,000 worth of custom-made furniture from Small and Boyes. Meanwhile Kinsella, Hugh Harris, and Jerry Lampert set about plotting to win the next election. Kinsella had an agenda to discuss with Bennett: "When I came out in 1981 . . . I thought it was important that we really get into poll-

ing. Polling in British Columbia was really non-existent."
At least the kind of polling Kinsella had in mind.

The first step was to sit down with Hugh Harris and
convince him to hire a couple of their buddies, Allan Gregg
and Ian McKinnon – Decima Research, the whiz-kid
pollsters for the Big Blue Machine. They were the hottest
pair of political number crunchers in the country, with an
impressive private-sector clientele and a talent for making
cross-country telephone lines sing. Back when Jerry Lampert was Joe Clark's executive assistant, McKinnon and
Gregg were graduate students working across the hall in
the Progressive Conservative research office. Gregg looks
like he's still on the cusp of adolescence with his tin grin
and punk haircut and a diamond stud in his ear. Ian McKinnon's dad, Allan, is the MP from Victoria and was minister
of defence in Joe Clark's burp of a government. Ian McKinnon had worked in the Privy Council Office and then in the
Prime Minister's Office.

The 1979 federal election that brought Joe Clark to
power changed political polling in Canada. Up until that
point the Liberals and Bill Bennett had Marty Goldfarb, and
the Tories relied on U.S. imports. "Up until the invention
of Allan Gregg," Hugh Segal remembers, "political polling
in Canada was based upon the American political schedule." If an election in Ontario or Canada or the West didn't
conflict with a presidential or congressional election, you
could get some good pollsters from the States. Otherwise,
the guys sent from Bob Teeter's Detroit operation, Market
Opinion Research, would arrive with other things on their
minds. Gregg was hired by the federal Tories in the 1979
general election. He worked directly for campaign chairman Lowell Murray as the link between party headquarters, Teeter's operation in Detroit, and Ronald Reagan's
pollsters, Decision Making Information, which was run by
Dick Wirthlin in California. Gregg had a computer terminal on his desk so he could remanipulate the data and
develop questions to elicit specific findings for his own
analysis. By all accounts he was brilliant. Following the
election he set up Decima Research as a joint venture that

included Gregg's mentor in the polling business, Dick Wirthlin. Wirthlin dropped out when he started working as a full-time pollster for Reagan. McKinnon came on board not long after.

When Patrick Kinsella and Jerry Lampert convinced Hugh Harris, who in turn convinced Bill Bennett, to take on Decima as the Socred party pollsters, the squeeze was put on Goldfarb. Harris and Goldfarb had not got on well from the beginning. According to Marty, much to Harris's annoyance, Bennett relied heavily on Goldfarb. After all, Marty got Bennett elected twice, in '75 and '79, when people thought it couldn't be done. Moreover, when Hugh Harris wanted to do something Bennett would say, "Sure. But you better check with Marty first."

Because Lampert and Kinsella wanted people they had dealt with in the past, Decima got the party work and Goldfarb retained his government polling contract. The differences in their work were infinitesimal except that the taxpayers paid the bill for Goldfarb, while Decima, we are told, was paid out of party coffers.

Hiring Decima was more than a change from Liberal to Tory pollsters; it was the beginning of the Socred experiment in political genetics, that seductive science that massages a voter's mind and transforms a politician's image. As Patrick Kinsella says: "Goldfarb only believes that he can take [a poll result] . . . and develop a strategy around it. And what we believe, we being Decima Research, [is] that you can take [poll results] . . . and we can change your mind. We can move you to do something that you may not have agreed on is the logical thing to do. . . . We can move you from one side of the ledger to the other."

The final member of the team of political geneticists was Toronto-based filmmaker Nancy McLean, one of the best political filmmakers in the country. McLean can turn Decima's dreams for its clients into celluloid reality; she can also make a politician relax in front of a camera. She has scrubbed and polished every Tory image from Robert Stanfield to Grant Devine to Brian Peckford. She made Joe Clark's 1980 campaign film, and in the 1981 Ontario cam-

paign she was Bill Davis's creative director for all media
and communications. Win some, lose some. By the beginning of 1982 she would have Bill Bennett buying his suits
with a little more care, clipping his locks a bit shorter,
taking a genuine interest in ties, and addressing the TV
camera with new makeup and confidence.

Two other technicians were already moving in to take up
their duties in Bill Bennett's West Coast laboratory: they
were Doug Heal and Norman Spector. Doug Heal, communications counsel in Information Services, took the helm of
what was to become a glitzy new government propaganda
machine. What had formerly been government information would now be information marketing. All government
press releases would be politically stroked before release;
all advertising contracts would be centrally controlled. The
voting public would no longer be told, they would be sold.
    Doug Heal was based in Toronto when he was recom-
mended for the job by an old Vancouver school chum and
fellow Liberal, Ron Basford. During his early years in the
business on the coast, Heal was a vice-president with
Wacky Bennett's favourite ad firm, James Lovick (now
Baker Lovick), and he managed to put in an hour or two
helping out Ron Basford with his political aspirations as
well as working for the Non-Partisan Association, the Socred civic farm team in Vancouver. Before his actual appointment, the Socreds had paid Heal $24,131 to draw up a
plan for the new information and advertising organization.
Not surprisingly, Heal's plan concluded that Doug Heal
was a perfect candidate to run the outfit. He got the job.
    Bennett didn't trust Heal and didn't want to use him.
Heal's public-service colleagues were cool toward the new
boy, who was expropriating their precious advertising budgets and public-relations machinery. This newest of deputy
ministers sullied his non-partisan title when he turned up
at a Socred party strategy session at Harrison Hot Springs, a
spa for the arthritic and the affluent in the Fraser Valley. As
if that wasn't enough, Heal called up a couple of old friends
to come up from Hollywood to help the Socreds improve

their image; never again would B.C.'s number one freedom fighter, Grace McCarthy, go in front of the cameras with frizzy hair. Leather-lunged Don Phillips would be restrained from reaching oratorical orgasm; and Bill Bennett would always appear freshly shaved. The tab for the Hollywood hotshots was $14,000. When the news of their work leaked to the press they were shipped back south for good.

Bennett liked the illusion that Heal was a benign lab assistant responsible to the provincial secretary; but by June 1981 the public service was nervous enough about Heal that they started leaking his memos. That was the final brick in the growing wall between Heal and Bennett. Heal was to languish in his office, misunderstood and unappreciated, until he was rescued by Kinsella well into the new year.

And finally there was Norman Spector. Young Dr. Spector, the thin, bearded, bespectacled academic who would translate the world for Bill Bennett, explain it to him in words of one syllable. Spector became assistant deputy minister and policy adviser to the Premier on the recommendation of Jim Matkin, deputy minister at Intergovernmental Relations. Bill Bennett had begun looking for a little intellectual artillery when, in 1981, it was his turn to be chairman of the premiers' committee. He had to slog through the constitutional debate. The first Quebec accord had already aborted, and the boys were back home with their tails between their legs. The chairman's job destroyed Manitoba's Sterling Lyon. B.C.'s Bill Bennett was determined it would not destroy him.

Bill Bennett sported Spector about the countryside like a jewel-encrusted watch fob or a new car. "This," he once told a member of the Ottawa press corps, "is Dr. Norman Spector. He is trilingual."

Spector had picked up French, English, Hebrew, and a working knowledge of Russian on his sparkly trip through academe. His family is in the textile business in Montreal. One of his schoolmates during his days at Talmud Torah Elementary School in Montreal was Hugh Segal; they still have a nodding acquaintance. While Segal attended the University of Ottawa, Spector was at McGill and managed to parlay his way into a coalition that won him a spot on the student council. He took his Master's degree in science, television, and radio at Syracuse University, picked up his Ph.D. in political science and public policy as a Woodrow Wilson Fellow at Columbia University, and took a spin through Hebrew University in Jerusalem. Spector's attempts to manipulate reporters in hopes of seeing his helpful hints as the next day's headlines have become a pastime for him. If he finds a reporter he can't manipulate, he plays the game the way his boss does and shuts him out.

Beginning in August 1981, Norman turned Bill Bennett's chamber-of-commerce view of the world into a legislative package that reflected the latest neo-conservative ideology. He did for Bennett, in Matkin's view, what Hugh Segal did for Bill Davis: he kept the government in line on policy development. He became, as well, Bennett's Metternich, his fixer, his quarterback in those close encounters with bristling trade unions, bubbling national issues, and the rabble in the streets. And sometimes, with amusing results, he helped Bill Bennett embellish his own pedestrian perceptions of how the world works.

On a warm sunny day in June 1982, Bill Bennett welcomed a crowd to the opening of the B.C. Festival of the Arts in Kamloops with a line lifted and twisted from Thomas Hobbes: "Without the arts," said Bennett, "the life of man is solitary, poor, nasty, brutish, and short." A few days later Bennett bumped into a cheerful reporter as he headed up the stairs to the legislature. "Mr. Bennett," the reporter said, "I'm surprised to see that you have been reading Leviathan." Bennett's response was reminiscent of that great Sweat Hog Vinnie Barbarino doing his incredulous "Whaaa?" Bennett was gone in a flash. An hour later the same cheery scribe happened upon Norman Spector. "Well, Norman," he said, "you have really done it now. You're giving Bennett stuff to say, and he doesn't have the foggiest idea what he's talking about." Norman was not happy to hear this. "No politician writes his own speeches, except for possibly Joe Clark." As the MLAs were waddling in for question period, the scribe encountered the Premier again. "What was that you were asking me about earlier?" he enquired. The scribe repeated the question; at which point Bennett trotted out a thirty-second précis of *Leviathan* that would have done any dustjacket proud.

"You have read it then?"

"Well, I've looked at it," Bennett allowed. Twenty-four hours later the quote of the day on the front page of the *Globe and Mail* was from B.C. Premier William Bennett, a line he used, we were told, to open the provincial arts festival. It began: "Without the arts . . ." Minutes later the scribe's phone rang. It was a guffawing Norman Spector. He, too, apparently reads the *Globe and Mail.*

By the time of Hugh Harris's sudden death in April 1982, the transformation was complete. Through Spector, Bennett was in firm control of policy and the senior public service. He was also being injected with the latest in neo-conservative language. When Norman Spector read Milton Friedman, Bill Bennett talked about the tyranny of the minorities; when Norman Spector picked up Mancur Olson, Bill Bennett started to make speeches about special-interest groups. The propaganda machinery was now operated by one button and one button pusher – the Premier. The population of B.C. was regularly polled, manipulated, and polled again. If they didn't believe the government they were hit with a barrage of advertising straight out of Bennett's new laboratory. If unemployment caused concern, Bill Bennett delivered bread and circuses, televised addresses, and handy scapegoats.

Hugh Harris's legacy was helping to turn a discombobulated bunch of up-country, West Coast loonies into a vital part of the urban, conservative strategy and talent network that spans the continent. He took Bill Bennett out of the country, and he assembled the parts for the Baby Blue Machine that would confidently clobber the NDP in 1983. In the words of Patrick Kinsella, it would be B.C.'s first taste of "high-tech politics."

4
TOUGH GUY

The insider's explanation of the genetic engineering that created the new Bill Bennett and his radical restraint program came to us quite by accident. On Wednesday, November 14, 1984, Patrick Kinsella entered a small, windowless lecture hall at Simon Fraser University's academic quadrangle in Burnaby, to give a speech on political marketing in the 1980s. Kinsella was flushed with victory: he was a campaign organizer for Brian Mulroney; he still had warm memories of the Socred campaign he had run in the spring of 1983. This man who gobbles poll results like a sugar-freak turned loose on Twinkies was here to show off his stuff.

At Kinsella's side was Peter Zeller, the president of the SFU Student Marketing Association. As Zeller got up to introduce Kinsella, someone in the front row clicked on a cheap hand-held tape-recorder. Neither Zeller nor Kinsella knew the recorder was on, and they certainly didn't expect that the crackling, barely audible tape recording of Kinsella's rambling discourse would be turned over to CBC television reporter Wayne Williams. It was a spellbinder.

There have always been questions about Bill Bennett's restraint crusade: what he intended to do, why he introduced it, and why he introduced it the way he did. In the closeness of room AQ 5008 Patrick Kinsella gave us the method and the motivation of a program that, in its attempt to rewrite the social contract for more than two and a half million people, has provoked years of turmoil and debate. Kinsella traced the restraint program to its roots: the polling that began in 1981, at about the time he was ordering that custom-made furniture:

> One of the things I persuaded the Premier to do, was to do what we call a base-line survey. Instead of a typical survey . . . of a two hundred or three hundred sample size, we wanted to do a massive sample, decreasing the margin of error, [and] therefore have a good idea as to what the people in British Columbia think. That was done [by Decima Research] in October of 1981, about two weeks after I arrived here. That poll told us, among other things, that there was a feeling out there that . . . things were starting to turn around. Actually, they were crumbling, they were going to dust if you'll remember. . . .
>
> We felt that we had to understand what it is that attracted voters to Bill Bennett and attracted voters to Dave Barrett . . . . It told us very clearly that David Barrett was far more popular, he was much more likable, i.e., he had a sense of humour. Most of the things about a leader that you like, David Barrett was it. He was friendly. He had good relationships with the media. Had a strong party to which he was truly the leader. There was no suggestion that anyone else wanted to be the leader. He was strong. He was perceived to be strong. He was frankly the guy that you would take to a Canucks game or take home to dinner. Bill Bennett, on the other hand, was perceived to be not a guy you would take to a Canucks game. He was seen to be a guy who was a strong businessman with very strong views on how things should be. Inflexible. A man who was perceived to be a strong leader, but had bad relationships with the press. Had bad relationships to some extent with his party, because there was always someone like a [Bill] Vander Zalm or someone who wanted to be God or king.
>
> So the [poll result] was very clear to us. Here was

Bennett on one hand, the premier, seen to be lacking in the sort of things that you may feel are necessary to be a leader. On the other hand, here was Dave Barrett who everyone liked. . . . So the problem we had was one of marketing. How do you market a guy who . . . is seen to be less friendly and less likable? . . .

We . . . developed a strategy that said in the event of a campaign whenever it is – '82 or '83 or '84 – what we've got to do is market Bill Bennett on the basis that in these tough economic times what we should be doing is having someone who is a tough guy leading us. More than ever before what you need now is a guy who understands that it's tough out there and he's tough as well. By contrast, surely now we don't need someone who thinks the whole thing's a joke. Now I know that that is taking it to extremes, but that's what we tried to get you to believe, if you will, as a voter in 1982-83. And it worked.

It worked for a couple of reasons. It worked because . . . we tried to contrast . . . the position that [Barrett] was trying to sell you on in 1982-83, that he was friendly, that he was likable, that he would be a good premier. Please try and forget about what I did from '72 to '75. I know I made some mistakes. But I was inexperienced. . . . I'm really a friendly guy and if you elect me premier again, I will not be the same sort of guy and I will make sure that the industry loves me.

And in 1982-83 David Barrett . . . would come and speak to anybody. . . . The audience could be four, or forty or four hundred or four thousand. But he would speak to anyone. And he'd dress up in his three-piece suit, and he would go to chambers of commerce and Rotary clubs and anyone who would listen to him, and he would give the theme that I am not the guy that I was. I will lead this province well. In 1972 if you recall what happened was that W.A.C. really in a sense defeated himself. And Barrett just let him do that. In 1983 what Barrett was trying to do was say now more than ever before we need a guy who is friendly, who can work with all kinds of people, who can go to chambers of commerce, and into the union halls, which Bill Bennett can't or won't. . . .

And what we were setting out to do was to make sure that everyone understood that Bill Bennett was perceived to be a leader, a tough guy in the sense that he knew that there had to be some tough decisions. And all of us have to make tough decisions at some point in our life, and Bill Bennett was trying to portray that into an election campaign.

And that was the beginning of restraint.

It was a marketing strategy. Government services would be chopped and channelled to complement Bill Bennett's Tough Guy image. Power and rights would be removed from children, tenants, school boards, minorities, and trade unions by a tough guy in tough times. The people of British Columbia would be set up to believe that what they needed was not some cuddly, humorous teddy bear with a heart, but a tough, inflexible son of a bitch they wouldn't be caught dead with at a Canucks hockey game. Toughness was sold as a virtue. Nice meant weak. Humour was a handicap. Restraint was a sado-masochistic exercise: The tougher Bill Bennett got, the better you felt.

Kinsella and his friends at Decima did the polling to come up with the Tough Guy image. It was Marty Goldfarb, however, still working on "issue polling" for the government, who developed the psychology Bennett would apply as the Tough Guy. Goldfarb called it "Tough Love", based on the heavy-duty American approach to rearing extremely difficult children. In a Tough Love family, if your kids are giving you a lot of problems, you severely discipline them by kicking them out of the house and by refusing to deal with them. This extreme action should shock them into changing their evil ways and make them come crawling home.

Kinsella had no trouble selling Bennett on the Tough Guy image strategy. It fit his politics. Goldfarb's Tough Love fit his personality.

Bennett once recounted a story about one of his four
sons, who left the Kelowna nest for Alberta. After a time
the boy called home: "Things are really pretty rough out
here. We're down to eating nothing but soup."

"Well," said Bill to his son, "phone me again when you
run out of soup."

Bill Bennett grew up believing that the welfare state
weakens individual initiative and dampens the en-
trepreneurial spirit. It was the same lesson his father had
taught to the Kelowna unemployed: You don't chop wood,
you don't get food. As premier, Bill loudly proclaimed:
"Economic development is the only social policy." But the
economic and social policies of the first eight years of his
government were inconsistent and often contradictory.
When he was first elected in 1975, he promised to cut back
on big government and control government spending. He
set up a ministry of deregulation for a few years and jacked
up user fees on the ferries and in government auto
insurance.

But he drifted from those first principles. Instead, he
spent almost as fast as the tax dollars rolled in. The public
service flourished. Through all the years of mini-boom
following the 1975 recession Bennett expanded his government's spending well beyond the rate of inflation. Relatively little was put aside for the inevitable crash that hits
resource-based economies. If Kinsella's 1980 poll results
were accurate, and people believed they were still living in a
booming economy in 1981, thank Bill Bennett for that
illusion. Government propaganda during the Kamloops by-
election promised never-ending prosperity and expanding
social programs, even though, as Kinsella knew, things
were "crumbling". Bill Bennett's expansionary policy was
driven by guilt and political expedience. In those days being
a tough guy didn't sell, so Bill Bennett expanded existing
programs and added new ones. To cover his operating
losses, he dug into reserves that were, ironically, partly a
legacy from the NDP government. And when times got
tough, he increased taxes.

Now, after years of paying lip-service to a welfare state

he didn't believe in, Bill Bennett could come out of the closet.

In early 1981 B.C.'s growth rate was higher and the unemployment rate was lower than the national average. But by August 1981, three months after the Kamloops by-election, Finance Minister Hugh Curtis was trying to "wring some fat out of the government". The recession was only beginning. By late 1981 B.C. Central Credit Union economists were predicting a $1 billion shortfall in the province's resource revenues. And as 1982 began, B.C. Telephone's in-house economist radically reduced his growth projections from 3 per cent to zero. By February 1982, provincial employment and growth trends had reversed. Inflation was roaring ahead. The business community was starting to put the heat on Bennett to avoid a deficit, a deficit that could only lead to tax increases for business.

However, putting the brakes on government spending would not be that simple. A few months earlier the teachers in British Columbia had received a wage increase of just over 17 per cent. This was particularly galling for Bennett. He already hated the teachers for helping to push Wacky from power. Now the number crunchers putting together their budgets were making the assumption that everyone in the public service would get 17 per cent that year. During the budget-making sessions, the solution put to Bennett and Treasury Board was simple: cut programs.

Bennett had a better idea: control public-sector wage increases. This would be much easier to sell politically. Nobody likes civil servants; everyone knows bureaucrats are overpaid and underworked. Besides, two major public-sector contracts were being negotiated: with the 40,000-member B.C. Government Employees' Union, the BCGEU, and the 24,000-strong Hospital Employees' Union, the HEU. The BCGEU was just coming off three years at 8 per cent each and was feeling feisty. The union's bargaining slogan was "Catch Up, Keep Up"; they would expect about 14 per cent. The hospital workers were about to reject an offer of 13.8 per cent in wages and benefits and opt for binding arbitration.

Bill Bennett didn't want to face the BCGEU or the HEU across the bargaining table. And he did not like arbitrated settlements. They tend to split the difference, and that was more than Bill Bennett wanted to give up. He needed a solution that would attack what he saw, in his nascent neo-conservative state of consciousness, as the biggest problem facing his government: civil-service wages and, ultimately, all union wages.

The bureaucrats countered that there was no authority for wage controls. The only option, once the possibility of arbitration was ruled out, was a zero increase, and that would violate free collective bargaining. With 46 per cent of the work force in the province in trade unions, you don't mess with that and hope to win an election.

At this point Kinsella's marketing strategy and Bill Bennett's chamber-of-commerce vision of society came together in heavenly harmony. In the bowels of the laboratory Dr. Kinsella began to create the Tough Guy. Within weeks he took his first steps.

In early January 1982, Kinsella summoned all cabinet ministers to a retreat at Schooner Cove, a sybaritic way-station of Jacuzzis, fireplaces, and tennis courts north of Nanaimo at Nanoose Bay. When the orders went out, the Tough Guy was on holiday, working on his drop-shots and serve. He was also licking his wounds, for he had not had a good fall season. He had been the premiers' chairman at the national constitutional debate in Ottawa. But even with Norman Spector holding his hand, when it got down to the short strokes, he was elbowed out of the way by Alberta's Peter Lougheed and Ontario's Bill Davis. "I was," he confessed, "chairman in name only." So much for a national profile.

When the Schooner Cove retreat was planned in the late fall of 1981 it was to be one of those crunchy-granola, blue-sky sessions to pull the cabinet and senior government officials together and contemplate the wonder of it all. The budget was not on the agenda: if Bill Bennett and his finance minister, Hugh Curtis, knew they were in trouble, they weren't admitting it.

Bennett just scoffed when economists told him that he had vastly overestimated his revenues, that his budget was a joke. At a press conference to discuss a quarterly financial report late in 1981, Curtis bobbed and weaved and waffled, but never answered the question: "Minister, are we in a recession?"

In most jurisdictions this is not considered a trick question. "Well," muttered Curtis, "I think we're in a difficult period. I have some difficulty determining what is a recession and what is a downturn." A recession, as even first-year economics students define it, is two consecutive quarterly downturns in gross product.

"But are we," the reporter persisted, "in a recession?"

"That," said the minister, planning his escape route, "is a matter of opinion."

The government had developed a pathological fear of uttering certain words, and "unemployment" and "deficit" topped the list. Saying "recession" would make it so; acknowledging it seemed like admitting to cheating on your wife.

By the time Schooner Cove rolled around, the cabinet mood was somewhere between consensus and collective panic. Treasury Board meetings to set the budget were going nowhere. Ministers were told to bring their own booze; lunch would be restricted to sandwiches. On the first day of the retreat Bennett explained that the meeting was an opportunity for the "cabinet to get its collective head around the policies that will emanate from the government's ability to finance for the next two to three years." In short, they had money problems.

The Schooner Cove meeting was supposed to be secret. The first leak was clocked out at four and a half minutes after the memo about the meeting hit a certain minister's desk. In the end the press was allowed on the property, but Bennett put his ministers' lips off limits. Reporters had to clear all interviews through the Tough Guy.

The first Schooner Cove press release fed to the media lounge lizards announced a province-wide enumeration of voters. The $5 million procedure would be completed by July. Could an election be far behind?

Throughout the three days of meetings, ministers and their deputies were to consider funding for programs outside of their own ministries. Brainstorming. It was a first for most ministers. Most of the sessions were led by the bureaucrats from the finance ministry; as information or bodies were needed, they were delivered from Victoria.

On the second day Jim Matkin turned up. He had been deputy minister of labour in the NDP government and, for a time, with the Socreds; he was also a lyricist of the latest rendition of the B.C. Labour Code. He was at Schooner Cove to argue for a wage-control program that left room to bargain. At the end of a long debate, Matkin had his mandate. He would develop a program of controls that covered all public-sector workers and set limits on wage increases of between 8 and 14 per cent.

This was to become the Compensation Stabilization Program (CSP). The combination of wage controls and government-spending controls would first confound and then defeat the NDP in the 1983 election. Yet, at the end of the three-day session the press had no inkling of what was hatched at Schooner Cove. The public was still wrestling with the image of Bill Bennett and his cabinet getting "its collective head" around government money problems.

In early February 1982 Bennett took his show on the road before he opened at home. At a first ministers' conference on the economy he tried to sell his wage-restraint program to the rest of the country, but only Pierre Trudeau gave him a sympathetic ear. Trudeau offered another voluntary hit of wage and price controls. At the conclusion of the meeting René Lévesque casually exhaled that Bennett was hot for wage controls because he was heading into negotiations with his public service; no one else had that immediate problem.

The cool reception from the other premiers sent Bennett off in an evangelical passion, more determined than ever to lead the way, to spread the word, to set a national example –

and to regain the spotlight usurped by Lougheed and Davis during the constitutional debate.

As 7:00 P.M. approaches on February 18, 1982, a nervous buzz runs through the BCTV studios. Bill Bennett has arrived: he has requested free television time. The subject is a matter of speculation. An election seems unlikely, so it is probably something to do with the economy. The Tough Guy will go on live, starring in a Patrick Kinsella production. After Bennett speaks, reporters will be able to ask penetrating questions, on live TV, for at least six minutes. The script is by the Tough Guy's policy guru, Norman Spector. Location manager is Patrick Kinsella, who chose television over the legislature because it's better marketing. Bill Bennett is led into the room, posed sitting on the edge of a desk, one foot on the ground, just so. He has been rehearsing for days. Once Bennett looks comfortable, Spector moves off to the control room and paces, sucking discreetly on a cigarette, pondering the angles of the shots on the monitors.

In a studio down the hall from Bennett and the reporters, "Newshour" is coming to an end. Three men wait to be positioned on slightly elevated platforms to respond to whatever it is Bill Bennett is about to say: Bill Hamilton, head of the Employers' Council of British Columbia, former postmaster general in the Diefenbaker cabinet; Jim Kinnaird, president of the B.C. Federation of Labour, former associate deputy minister of labour in the NDP government; and Dave Barrett, leader of the Opposition and former premier.

The lights come up on Bennett, and a floor director throws him his cue. He is calm; at times, almost animated. His makeup is even; his suit well fitted. "I am taking this unusual step of speaking to you this evening," he begins, "to outline some of the measures the government will pursue to strengthen our economy." He is at ease with the classical elements. Like his father, he battles the federal government with one hand and beats off the Socialist

Hordes with the other; maintaining the polarization is a matter of political survival.

First Ottawa: "Today our people are frustrated by the absence of national leadership." In the next breath he lunges at the socialists: "Our last recession in 1975 [when the NDP was in power] was, for the main part, internal to British Columbia; for at that time our province – even with its bountiful natural advantages – actually was performing worse than the Canadian and United States economies. Our unemployment rates were higher and levels of growth lower, which gave us room to manoeuvre and allowed us to climb out of recession by getting our house in order. . . . So that today we are performing better than the Canadian and U.S. economies."

His delivery is smooth. His statistics and recollection of history are wanting.

In fact, in February 1982, while Bill Bennett is speaking to the people on TV, inflation in the lower mainland is at 12.97 per cent; the Canadian average is 11.6 per cent. B.C.'s unemployment rate is 9.2 per cent and climbing. (It was 8.5 per cent in 1975.) The Canadian average is 8.8 per cent – seasonally adjusted, of course.

Once the posturing is out of the way, Bennett moves to the meat of his message. The Tough Guy will smite inflation and high interest rates by limiting government spending to match revenue and by curbing public-sector wage increases. A neo-conservative prescription worthy of Ronald Reagan and Margaret Thatcher. He will lead the nation. Months will pass before Trudeau comes in with his own six-and-five plan. (Three years after Bennett's speech, governments in Canada and the United States will still be amassing record deficits while interest rates and inflation will have declined dramatically. But don't look for logic.) Bennett's solution limits wage increases to 8-14 per cent, outrageously generous by 1985 standards, but just keeping up with inflation in 1982. Spending increases on everything from Crown corporations to hospitals, municipalities, and schools will be held to a maximum of 12 per cent.

The program would go into effect immediately and remain in place for two years. More than 200,000 workers, one in six, would be hit. "Collective bargaining in the public sector," Bennett purrs, "will take place in the normal manner." Except for one minor point: if the settlement is too rich, it will be rolled back. And Bill Bennett would appoint the guy to do just that, a veteran of the private and public labour-arbitration wars, Ed Peck. While Ottawa and the NDP Opposition ponder Bennett's characteristic rebukes, the Tough Guy wraps up his speech with a call for co-operation. These measures will not work "unless all British Columbians are prepared to work with them." He also promises that, despite the program of restraint, "we cannot and will not turn our backs on those most in need in our society." This is strong medicine to be sure, he concludes, but it is "the only alternative to the damaging policies now being pursued nationally."

The press questions that follow Bennett's speech get tangled in the minutiae of an announcement reporters have had no time to consider. Within a few minutes the TV audience is moved down the hall to Hamilton, Kinnaird, and Barrett.

First up is Bill Hamilton, the calm voice of business. He is understandably cheery: Tough Guy, you are singing my song. Hamilton's faith would take some time to fail.

Next, Jim Kinnaird, the gritty voice of labour, has this bit of eloquence: "To hell with him as far as I'm concerned. . . . I'd go after his guts for doing this sort of thing. None of the provinces have wage and price controls. . . . We'll give him a confrontation on this one." (Jim Kinnaird died suddenly of a heart attack on February 17, 1983, almost one year to the day after making that promise.)

Finally there is the leader of Her Majesty's Loyal Opposition. It is, for Barrett, the beginning of eighteen months of evasion on restraint in government spending and public-sector wage controls. He denounces the program as a cynical election ploy, then rants on about Patrick Kinsella's custom-made furniture. All $15,000 worth. Some restraint.

The following day, as Kinsella prepares a press release announcing he is cancelling his furniture order, Bill Bennett delivers the gospel to the Vancouver Board of Trade. (A film crew is shooting footage to ship back to Toronto for Nancy McLean, the Blue Machine image polisher and film producer.) The boys from the board eat it up; but B.C. economists give the message mixed reviews. Two of them, John Helliwell, a resource economist from UBC, and Richard McAlary, chief economist for the B.C. Central Credit Union, predict that the program will lead to increased unemployment, particularly if it means shutting down or delaying capital projects. Michael Walker, the maven of monetarism and the head of the right-fisted Fraser Institute says, that while unemployment is of some concern, project cancellation will not come for eight to ten months. By that time the U.S. economy will have turned around and will drag B.C. with it. He is right and he is wrong; the U.S. economy does turn, but B.C. is left in its dust. Both Walker and Helliwell take a shot at Bennett for not saving money when times were good. Walker points out that the government has been spending more than it has been taking in for two years and spending has been going up by 17 and 18 per cent.

In the aftermath of Bill Bennett's February 18 announcement, Southam News veteran economics commentator Don McGillivray writes: "The pity is that wage restraint, especially in the public sector, is almost completely irrelevant. First, it's aimed at inflation, which is no longer the major problem confronting the economy. Second, we have fresh evidence from the behaviour of the Canadian economy itself over the past four years that wage restraint doesn't cure inflation. The main problem in Canada right now is a spreading and deepening recession. . . . Tighter restraint policies now can only deepen the recession." The independent Conference Board of Canada would look at what Bill Bennett's policies were doing and finally agree. But McGillivray is one of the few journalists not totally consumed by the rhetoric of restraint, the language of the new economic order, which makes less government a virtue and special-interest groups a plague on the backside of society.

Eight days after the Tough Guy delivers his opening shot, his finance minister announces that the government is interested in consultation. Better late than never. Three days after the finance minister's announcement we are introduced to a new glitzy slogan and symbol created by Doug Heal, minister of propaganda and marketing. Doug is no longer in the doghouse. He has taken the B.C. provincial flag first introduced by Wacky back in 1960 and given it a designer twist. Jordache flag B.C. To it he has added the slogan: "That's the B.C. Spirit!" – an upper-lip stiffener in Nouveau Socred red, white, and blue. The flag, the slogan, or both soon begin to appear on everything from the main smokestacks of the B.C. Ferry fleet, to the faces of the clocks in government liquor stores. A more extensive advertising campaign is in the works.

Bennett's TV announcement, with or without the designer flag, set off a series of explosions around the province. For the people who ran schools, hospitals, and municipalities it was a matter of crisis management. Bill Bennett created the crisis. Everyone else had to try and manage. School boards had a 17 per cent wage increase to deal with; layoffs were inevitable. The program that pledged to "strengthen the British Columbia economy" began by putting people out of work. The head of the B.C. Teachers' Federation predicted that 4,000 teachers would lose their jobs. The minister of education said the man was over-reacting, that the figure was closer to 1,000 or 1,500. Three years later, teachers are still getting the axe, and 4,000 teaching positions have been eliminated. The head of the B.C. school trustees, though a closet Socred, was forced to protest: "This is a very real attack on the standards of education in this province. . . . We are facing a very large problem, and I don't think it has been thought through by the government." Hospital administrators figured that even if their workers were limited to an 8 per cent increase in wages, a 12 per cent ceiling on hospital budget increases would mean staff laid off and beds shut down. Municipalities were stuck with paying their workers the 15 per cent they won in the last contract and holding cost increases to 12 per cent. Vancouver announced an immediate hiring freeze. Municipal services would be cut across the province.

There was, however, some comic relief. On February 16, two days before the Tough Guy took to the tube to put the brakes on government spending and wage increases, Alayne Falle, an "accounting clerk 3" in Consumer and Corporate Affairs turned in her letter of resignation. For the past ten months she had been smuggling out photocopies of ministry documents that detailed the decidedly unrestrained spending habits of her minister, Peter Hyndman. Hyndman, a Tory blue blood who can trace his ancestry to the first chief justice of Prince Edward Island, had a brother in Peter Lougheed's cabinet; his wife, Vicky, is Junior League.

Falle handed over a foot-thick stack of material to her local NDP MLA, initiating what proved to be the biggest security rupture in B.C. political history. Shortly after Falle's resignation, the documents surfaced in the hands of Vancouver *Sun* reporters, who asked pointed questions of Hyndman about his exotic dinners and "working vacation" at public expense. The press and the Opposition had a field day chronicling Hyndman's excesses and excuses in the face of government cutbacks to essential social services, education, and health. The RCMP investigated and found nothing illegal. The auditor general audited and gave Peter a "public spanking". The Opposition fulminated, Bill Bennett procrastinated, and, finally, Peter Hyndman resigned, ending a promising political career.

Within weeks of his February 18 announcement Bennett knew that he had boxed himself in. The economy was crumbling faster than he could admit publicly. His April budget was falling apart, and for the third year in a row he was running an operating deficit. His estimates for forestry revenues had the Council of Forest Industries and International Woodworkers of America (IWA) economists shaking their heads in amazement.

There also seemed to be some difference between what he had said he was going to do and what he actually did. He may not have been raising taxes, but he was definitely hiking user fees for a long list of government services. He had promised not to "compromise the high standards of services to the needy and elderly of British Columbia"; but then he knocked the front teeth out of the Denticare program. (The rest would be pulled within a year.) Two out of three senior citizens in the province were affected.

Bennett's spending ceilings were much too high to balance his budget. The hospital workers and the B.C. Government Employees' Union, both negotiating contracts, had been left with expectations far higher than the government could afford, given their spending priorities. The BCGEU would have been happy with 8 to 14 per cent. They believed they'd been given assurances – nudge, nudge, wink, wink – that they'd get close to 14 per cent. The Tough Guy's formula for restraint was about to become an equation for acrimony and confrontation.

Bennett's general revenue projections were based on two assumptions: U.S. interest rates would fall and inflation would decline, immediately. He was hoping for a turnaround by September 1982, just in time for an election. However, interest rates and inflation kept moving up.

By May 1982, when he was asked about spending ceilings and wage controls, Bennett said, "I'm not going to work to any figures." On May 10, he rose in the legislature to say: "The public perhaps misunderstood the compensation stabilization program. They have thought because we said '10 per cent is a ceiling; plus or minus 2 per cent is a ceiling,' that perhaps there was a floor and ceiling between 8 per cent and 12 per cent. They are incorrect: there is no floor. We have a flexible ceiling." The restraint program sounded like a rubber room. The Tough Guy sounded like he should be in one.

By the middle of May, B.C. hospitals had laid off 2,100 workers and shut down 1,200 beds. Doctors were predicting that by midsummer people would be dying because of lack of facilities. There was still no word about the arbitrated settlement for hospital workers, but Bennett was threatening to bring in tough legislation to ensure that wage settlements did not lead to job losses or program cuts, a clever strategy to put the unions on the defensive. The chief negotiator for the province's hospitals said that Bennett's demands would be impossible to meet if an arbitrated settlement came in at 8 per cent or more. Norman Spector moved into the spotlight for the first time to warn all arbitrators that they must curb the size of their awards. Spector said that the government would overturn any arbitration that resulted in layoffs or cuts in service.

On May 25, another bulletin was issued by the custodians of the Rubber Room. Bill Bennett's wage-restraint program, with no floor and a flexible ceiling, moved into the fourth dimension: all wage settlements would have to be "within the employer's ability to pay". Ultimately "ability to pay" would be the sole deciding factor. And, of course, Bill Bennett's control over budgets and transfer payments to government institutions and Crown corporations determined that "ability".

In July, Bennett sliced another $60 million from the education budget. Beleaguered school boards across the province were spending virtually all their time writing and rewriting budgets to suit new government guidelines. Education took a back seat to number crunching. The Burnaby school board calculated that all the fiddling with figures had cost almost $80,000 in bureaucrats' time. The Surrey board put it at $100,000, not including time donated by principals, department heads, and teachers.

Meanwhile BCGEU negotiations were going nowhere. The government didn't want to talk money. John Fryer, the union's chief negotiator, called for a strike vote to give the bargaining committee a little more clout. Rumours began to circulate that Bennett was going to lower the ceiling on his Rubber Room again; his deficit had tripled, to more than $1 billion. Two hours after the BCGEU announced their overwhelming mandate for a strike, Bennett lowered the ceiling.

Bennett and Spector became directly involved in the negotiations, first in private meetings with Fryer, then across a table with Fryer and union president Norm Richards. The government's negotiator was reduced to a messenger. The money message was 6 per cent – Trudeau's guideline. Fryer asked for mediation. Finally his 40,000 union members walked out, in the first province-wide public-sector strike in B.C. history. Bennett once again took to the airwaves with one of his dad's best tactics. He said he was being flooded with phone calls from BCGEU rank and file who wanted to accept the government offer. Fryer called his bluff and took a vote on the offer. "Do you want 6 per cent?" A resounding "No!"

However, the union strategy was reduced to rotating strikes. Bennett had public opinion on his side; in the end there was no catch up and no keep up. The settlement was a hybrid of just over 6 per cent in money, $200 in government bonds, and a loose and organic formula for productivity increases that perfectly suited Bennett's portrayal of a slack-assed public service. While Norman Spector did the spadework on the settlement, the Tough Guy was there for the kill. He shook hands with the union leadership and smiled for the cameras. Perfect politics. Perfect marketing. The product was catching on.

5

THAT'S THE B.C. SPIRIT!

Each afternoon, when the legislature is in session in Victoria, MLAS rise for the prayer. Bill Bennett pushes into the chamber through the revolving doors on the government side of the house and, as is his custom, glances up at the small notice board to catch the name of the visiting man of God. On September 29, 1982, it is the Reverend Ronald Johnstone. As members bow heads and close eyes, the Reverend begins: "Almighty God, we thank you that you have called us, and the people of British Columbia have elected us to be members of the Legislature. . . . May there be peace on earth; may it begin with me. Courage is what we need – courage to carry out the mandate which has already been given to us, rather than the spending of money on an election few citizens want."

Bill Bennett desperately wanted to call an election in the fall of 1982. He was more than three years into his five-year term. The economy, he suspected but wouldn't admit, was going to get worse before it got better. His own popularity would fare the same. The Baby Blue Machine was tuned up and purring in the driveway. Bennett ached to put the pedal to the metal, to get out there and charm the socks off those voters. But, because of bad numbers in the polls, a greedy but aborted attempt at gerrymandering, and a loss of nerve, or divine intervention, the Tough Guy choked.

Nothing would gel. He expected the government workers' strike to last longer than it did; that would have given him the issue he needed. He baited the union leadership with his version of Dad's meat-cleaver strategy: foreign devils with their foreign ideas were leading a wholesome homegrown union membership astray. Early in September, Bennett pouted, "John Fryer [the union's British-born chief negotiator] brings a whole bag of tricks from Britain on how to deal with industrial relations that I just am not equipped to deal with."

Bennett dispatched Decima to poll the depths of the B.C. psyche. He announced, a bit late, a cheap-mortgage-money scheme to help homeowners who had survived 20 per cent-plus interest rates a year earlier. Then he instructed Baby Blue Machine chief mechanic Jerry Lampert to set up nomination meetings to take place around the province as soon as the writ was dropped. The tour buses were ordered, renovated, and painted red, white, and blue.

Doug Heal, father of the designer flag and "That's the B.C. Spirit!", put together a massive television advertising campaign and started buying TV time slots. Total cost: $443,000. There was "A Plan for Economic Recovery in British Columbia", a $100,000 brochure wrapped in flags and slogans promising strong leadership, a "simplified government", and better days ahead through government "action".

Two of B.C.'s local business journals were flooded with full-page ads from government ministries and Crown corporations. They responded with objective feature stories on the wonders being wrought by Social Credit. (The NDP were apparently unavailable for comment.) Doug Heal liked the fifty-six page centre section of the October 18 issue of *Construction West* (circulation 14,000) so much that he bought a 10,000 copy print run, which was then distributed via government centres throughout B.C.

The ads were a delightful blend of facts and fibs. The

most obvious fib dealt with the Socred mythology that none of the megaprojects, from north-east coal to B.C. Place, the massive redevelopment and domed stadium in downtown Vancouver, would cost the taxpayers of B.C. a cent. Of course, no social services would suffer as a result of Bill Bennett's Edifice Complex. One bit of full-page fluff on B.C. Place claimed that the project that was still rising out of the mud at False Creek was "already paying its way". The ad had been running for three months when Stephen Rogers, the minister responsible for the project, confessed that the $205 million for the project was being fronted by a Crown corporation, B.C. Building Corporation. Interest on debt repayment amounted to $30 million in the first year. This direct drain on the central treasury presumably affected how much the government could allocate to health, education, and welfare. Moreover, no money-making event had ever been held on the site. What, one was forced to wonder, did the government mean when it claimed the project was "already paying its way"? Well, said Rogers, "What does it mean? Is it an expression? I guess that's the best way to put it."

Then there was gerrymandering. Darril Warren, an old political opponent whom Bill had whipped almost a decade earlier in the Kelowna by-election to replace Wacky, was appointed head of a government commission on electoral reform. Warren produced a report that would clear the way for the government to add half a dozen new seats, mostly in Socred strongholds. Warren believed in taking representation by population a step further: he wanted the geographical size of a riding to influence the number of its elected members. One mountain – one vote. Bill loved it.

It was all there for an election: the ad campaign, the promises, the issue. But then the plan came unhinged: the foreign devils running the government employees' union settled their dispute. The attempt to implement the Warren report was viewed as naked political greed. The Tough Guy was forced to withdraw the bill and all thoughts of an election. Just as well: the education issue was flaring up again over budget cuts. In fact, the restraint announced in February 1982 was putting the squeeze on people already down because of a failing B.C. economy.

Just as kids were heading back to school, Education Minister Bill Vander Zalm paused from picking the wings off flies and deprecating bilingual cornflakes boxes to enforce the government's deepening commitment to cutbacks in the education system. "I think," he opined, "a person has to be able to write good." They would, however, "write good" with fewer tools: fewer pencils, fewer books, fewer teachers. Pink slips were flooding the province; in Vander Zalm's own riding of Surrey, sixty temporary teachers were chopped, and others would follow. Remedial summer courses were cancelled. Adult basic-education classes would be wiped out. Enrolment in programs to encourage kids to pick up grade 10 was frozen. School counselling was trimmed, as were field trips, music courses, and French immersion. If you wanted to *parlez-vous*, you could just read your cereal box.

The rest of the province was no better off.

Kamloops, in the sage-covered hills of south-central British Columbia, eighteen months after the May 1981 by-election and government promises of continued prosperity: it is a community in crisis. This is cattle country, a freight centre; it has sawmills, pulp. The depression hangs about, impervious and unavoidable, like the early morning fog that hugs the Thompson River Valley in October.

On May 10, 1981, Bill Bennett had hauled himself up in front of three hundred people at a Kamloops Chamber of Commerce rubber-chicken luncheon to tell the good burghers how to send the "right" message to potential investors by voting Socred in the imminent exercise in democracy. "B.C. is riding a very prosperous tide," he had said, "and we're doing it against the trend of the rest of North America. It doesn't have to stop." At the time, Employment Canada had 4,749 UIC claims in Kamloops. Now, in September 1982, the claims stand at 9,387. Double.

The number of free food hampers distributed by the

church-organized food bank in October 1982 is up. To pick up the hampers, some people drive the sixty kilometres south from Barrier, joining those sent by social workers because provincial welfare payments are inadequate. Suicides are up; so is the number of old people caught shoplifting.

Afton Mines hasn't produced a nickel's worth of copper, gold, or silver since more than three hundred men were laid off in July. Balco Industries is down to one shift in its sawmill, and the Evans operation at Savona is down from two hundred people to fifty.

What is up is welfare payments. Business is brisk. A year earlier the Kamloops area office handled 2,280 cases; it is now up to 3,237.

Liquor sales are up marginally, but doctors' tempers are up considerably. Some who thought the $30 million payback out of medicare fees to the Socreds was a good idea a month ago have changed their minds. The number of people visiting doctors is down by 15 per cent. Most who do are in a decided funk over work or money or a lack of both. To make matters worse, many of them no longer have medical coverage; it went with the job. Doctors working in emergency situations are writing off 25 per cent of their fees as bad debts. Dentists are losing patients, particularly seniors and kids under fourteen. One of the first programs the Socreds cut was Denticare.

Business is also down at dry-cleaning stores and building-supply outfits. At Irly Bird, they tell you, "It's a heck of a lot slower than last year." The local army recruiting officer says, "It's a buyer's market." More people are coming through the door, but fewer are being signed up. There's no life like it, particularly when the bottom has fallen out of the economy. The normal turnover in the armed forces has dropped right off.

For some reason the hair-cutting business is holding up, and the fitness program at the YWCA is selling like hotcakes. It is cheap, it is fun, and it is definitely not fattening.

Because of all the kids out of work, college enrolment will go up until the government cuts funding for post-secondary schools and wipes out student bursaries. Public-school enrolment is down because parents are clearing out for cheaper parts. Going home to the folks; rolling out the cot in the spare room; insulating the garage.

Construction is down. The once-booming Aberdeen Hills development is bust; building permits issued by the city are at about one-third of last year's level. Work in the building trades is dead. Grim winter is coming.

The single-resource-based towns that spawned the polarization in B.C. politics at the turn of the century continue to dominate the economic climate of the province. There is still a species of British Columbian that avoids the big cities and makes his way across the province from one boom and inevitable bust to the next. But by the fall of 1982 there are few places left to go.

Even around Cranbrook in the south-east, where action in the coal fields still keeps unemployment figures single-digit, the recession is taking its toll. As soon as north-east coal came on stream and the Japanese buyers could whip-saw the coal companies over price and sales volumes, the bottom fell out here, too.

Check out the scene at the welfare office; then drift over to the legal-services society a couple of blocks away. See the lunacy of government cuts to legal aid. There is a new kind of client coming around for welfare cheques. Here is a man who has worked all his adult life and who firmly believes that people on welfare are a bunch of bums being paid well for doing nothing. He wanders up to the government building once, twice, hangs out by the door for a half-hour or so. Finally, he gets it together to fill out an application form.

What infuriates this humbled fellow even more than his past rants about the welfare bums? Welfare isn't enough to live on. It certainly isn't enough for his mortgage payments or to get his tools out of hock so he can look for work. The welfare people check what he still owns: "Sell it or you can't get welfare." He says, "How can I sell my car or my boat? Nobody wants to buy this stuff. Nobody wants to buy anything."

He's offered $750 a month. What he needs is $10,000

right now. He becomes a case, a number in a system that is bursting at the seams. Last year he could have seen a social worker within three days. Now it takes three weeks. Four workers handle nine hundred cases. In Cranbrook the case-load is up more than 54 per cent since 1981; most of these new cases are defined as "employable". The emergency funds that were supposed to last until the end of March 1983 have been handed out by the middle of October 1982.

The number of battered wives turning up at shelters in Cranbrook has tripled in the past three months. What's happening with kids is even worse. People are coming to the welfare office and just saying, "Here, take my kids. I can't handle them any more."

As the social fabric of this community shreds under the weight of the recession, more people flock to the legal-aid office. But look what you find there: applications are up by 20 per cent, but the staff has been chopped in half because of budget cuts. Money is being diverted to build megaprojects – like north-east coal, the development that put an even tighter squeeze on the people in Cranbrook. Legal assistance that once came free has either disappeared or, at best, will cost you a $30 user fee. Some of the hardest hit are women and their kids. For many of them legal aid was the way to get a maintenance settlement through family court. That legal assistance will now be denied. Welfare, inevitably a bigger drain on the provincial treasury, becomes the alternative.

At the very centre of the province, in Prince George, there is a change. More than winter is moving in. Skittering along the streets, avoiding frozen puddles, you notice that the smell belching from the town's three pulp mills is not quite as acrid as it once was. The distinctive odour one Socred politician once called "the smell of money", has faded. Two of the mills shut down in late October for at least a month. Pulp markets are soft because newspapers aren't as thick as in better times. Then the Swedes devalued the krona. Swedish pulp prices dropped on the world market; B.C. sales fell and stockpiles rose. At least half a dozen sawmills had no market for their chips and were forced to shut down and wait. More than 2,000 men and women were out on the streets.

Even before that shutdown Prince George had close to 20 per cent unemployment, a record for the province and a title they usually armwrestle Kamloops for. The biggest increase is among men between twenty-four and forty-four, the group that was never supposed to be unemployed. As of October 13, 1982, the number of Prince George residents on unemployment insurance is 97 per cent higher than a year earlier. Welfare statistics have jumped from 5,200 cases to 7,400 cases. Wife beating, of course, is a growth industry.

If you want some good news, wedge your way into the new library; it's doing a booming business. And the local video rental outlet is packed with couples looking for an alternative form of cheap entertainment. The usual pastime has given Prince George the highest birthrate per capita in Canada. "You get a bit blasé about it after you've been up here for a while," one blasé maternity ward nurse allows. Another baby boom is being planned for, nine months after the pulp mills shut down.

The latest mining-industry casualty of the depression lies two hours west of Prince George at Fraser Lake. Follow the Yellowhead Highway as it winds through the gently rolling hills of the Nechako River Valley, past stands of poplar and fields of golden stubble where beef cattle and fat horses share what is left with the flocks of Canada geese on their way south.

Fraser Lake, a town of mostly modern, well-kept bungalows, sits up against the highway and covers a sun-soaked bench on the south shore of the lake. A stone's throw east along the shore is the Fraser Lake Saw Mill, one of two economic engines that drive this community of 1,600 people. To the west and south is the Endako Mine site. Until early October 1982, it was the world's largest producer of molybdenum, a substance used in making steel. That mine is the reason most people came here, and Endako employed almost six hundred. Now there's a glut of molybdenum on the market. Just a skeleton crew of sixty-five is left.

The death of the mine came slowly. In March 1981, fifty people were laid off. In June the owner, Placer Development Ltd., shut the mine down for three months. Most people took holidays and figured on a September 7 start-up date. In mid-August Placer announced that the mine would be down until mid-1983. Single people started to drift away, looking for work or just going back home.

Angus Davis, the mayor of Fraser Lake, is one of the people who lost his job. He stopped working as a personnel supervisor at Endako and went on half salary as a security guard. On September 3 he was laid off. Six weeks later Endako announced that the site would close "indefinitely". Angus and those buddies who were still around filled their days doing chores, splitting wood, or helping friends.

"I'm not concerned, I'm confused," Angus says. When he first came up here from Nelson with his wife, Arlene, "I told myself I'd stay two years. Gradually you make your home here." They raised three kids. Two are still in school in the town. "Now you have to make a decision. You have to go." He will be gone within the year.

His friend Harold Johnson's story is not much different except he is close to retirement and will stay on in Fraser Lake. This is the second mine that has shut down on him. The first one was at Uranium City, Saskatchewan. When he came out here he figured he would never build a house in a mining town again. He built within two years. "The problem now," he says, "is that nobody knows how long it's going to be. If it was a year you could take up odd jobs."

Harry Toews has also been laid off. He was a welder up at the mine and isn't too worried. "People are very easily hooked on security. They shouldn't be. Not miners. Look at the history of this province. There are ghost towns everywhere." Harry is working a day a week at the sawmill and setting up his own small fabricating plant to tide himself over. He figures he'll get full-time work at the mill within three months.

More than half a million dollars that didn't go to Kamloops,

Cranbrook, Prince George, or Fraser Lake went into advertising in praise of Social Credit initiatives. Bennett may have choked on the election, but he wasn't going to waste the propaganda. The slick television ads were fronted by Fred Latremouille, a cute-as-pie rock jock turned weatherman on the province's most watched news program, BCTV's "Newshour". The man who won hearts and minds by telling them when to carry their umbrella or to head for the ski slopes was now flakking for the Tough Guy: "To quote Charles Dickens," said Fred, "we live in the worst of times. Canada's in an economic mess. Yet in some ways, here in B.C., we are approaching the best of times. Astonishing things are happening to create jobs now and in the future."

There were a few astonishing things about the commercials themselves. One spot about a government/industry job-creation program had to be pulled because the government involved was the federal government, not Victoria. A spot lauding job training for women in non-traditional jobs got the axe because the Socreds cut the funding to the program while the commercial was in production. A couple of other video vote-getters bit the dust before they were aired, because – you guessed it – the health care and education programs were chopped. Somebody forgot to tell the weatherman and the film crew. The few spots that remained were run and run again through the fall and into the new year. Doug Heal, architect of these sometimes-fictional essays, insisted to the final frame that the commercials softened up the voters for the election that would finally come in the spring of 1983.

The "Plan for Economic Recovery" was distributed as planned on October 7, the day the writ was originally going to be dropped. The liberties taken in the $100,000 brochure made the TV commercials seem scrupulous. There was a government promise of $125 million for job creation; but $100 million was a continuation of old programs or old money tarted up with new labels, and the other $25 million was mostly smoke and mirrors. The job-creation program to build a natural-gas pipeline to Vancouver Island was announced so frequently it deserved its own ministry.

This strategy of putting a new coat of paint on an old program or promise accelerated during the next few years until virtually every dollar spent by the government was defined first as "Job Creation", then "Job Action", and finally "permanent jobs in the private sector". The few real job-creation programs in place in 1982 were falling far short of the targets set by the Socreds. A plan that used unemployment-insurance funds, provincial money, and some private-sector dollars was supposed to create 10,000 jobs in the forest industry. The most liberal estimates of success came in at 3,800 jobs, while unemployment in the province was soaring.

When the Socreds first announced their job-creation initiatives in the spring of 1982 there were 126,000 people unemployed in B.C. Two months after the $100,000 brochure hit the streets, 193,000 were out of work; government restraint had wiped out more than 4,000 jobs from the ranks of the public service alone.

By this time, Bennett's pollsters were soothsaying full time. Decima Research was wading through the chicken guts for a possible election date, and came up with some startling findings: the deepening recession was causing fundamental changes in the way people viewed the world. Unlike the Great Depression, which led to a blossoming of social programs to assist the downtrodden, people in B.C. were becoming more selfish as times got tougher. Lean mean times were producing lean mean people. Just how lean and mean was being tested by Marty Goldfarb's Canadian Polling Institute. This was the basis for his Tough Love strategy. His poll questionnaire ran to twenty-six pages and covered everything from the government's restraint program to "legislation to further restrict the power and privileges of unions in B.C.", teachers' salaries, education funding levels, tuition fees, and the possibility of disbanding "organizations such as the Human Rights Commission" to save a few bucks. (This was all very interesting in light of what was to come six months down the road.) There was even a series of questions asking whether the government should "have the right to put commercials on television which show how their policies and programs are helping the taxpayer."

Meanwhile, Bill Bennett's economic recovery program was taking on a life of its own. When he first announced his restraint program to "strengthen" the B.C. economy, he described a two-year program of recovery. Nine months later, on November 24, 1982, he told 550 people at a Victoria Chamber of Commerce bun toss that "we're looking at a three-year period of recovery." On December 3, nine days later, he told a group of reporters, "We've got a five-year program for economic recovery, and we're the only government in Canada that has one."

This was nothing more than Bill Bennett revving his engine and listening for the misfires. The main thrust of his restraint program, the initiatives to cut programs and centralize power in Victoria, would not be hinted at until he crossed the finish line. He would have to wait, allow the propaganda, the TV commercials, and the brochure to cheer up the crowds and hope for a small swing in the polls and an issue to help him pull ahead and win the next election.

6

BILL JUST GRINNED

Bennett and his handlers played their election hand tight-lipped and tough. Bennett was sold as the boss man. He wasn't going to debate with the Opposition, because the Opposition didn't know what it was talking about. All you had to do was trust Bill Bennett. Don't worry your pretty little head about a lot of details like tax increases and service cuts – the Tough Guy was the right guy for tough times. He would take care of everything and give the rest of the country a lesson while he was at it.

For the first time in postwar history, the B.C. government was going to the people without a budget in place. Instead of calling the house together to approve interim spending before the fiscal year end, Bennett ran the province by order-in-council. This avoided giving the Opposition a forum for asking nasty questions. In fact, Treasury Board had the budget figured out months earlier: the government was going to end up in the hole. Finance Minister Hugh Curtis was taking elocution lessons to help get his mouth wrapped around the word "deficit". There were going to be massive program cuts in the passionate pursuit of a balanced budget, but none of this was what you wanted to announce before an election.

Bill Bennett refused to say more than that he was in a "pre-election mode". Patrick Kinsella tucked the latest poll results into his back pocket and led the Tough Guy around the province during February to try out a few new lines.

The pollsters said people wanted their governments to be "positive"; there was too much "negative" in their lives. So "positive" Bill Bennett was. On one occasion he brushed aside a scrum of reporters – no time to talk, he said: "I'm very busy in a positive way."

The extensive Tough Love poll conducted by Marty Goldfarb in the fall of 1982 gave Bennett confidence as he forged ahead with his lean, aggressive vision of government. You could almost see old Wacky there on the stump as Bill flexed his ideology. He would not be "seduced by those who would argue for greater government". Then he turned on the unions: "I've seen the loss of democracy in the workplace in this province," all because of union leaders "who got that power not because they earned it, but because they represent legitimate groups." (This was not a man concerned with logic.) They were part of the "noisy minorities", a "coalition of dissent", part of a foreign invasion of B.C. that was taking advantage of "the silent majority". "Many are already filtering west," he warned of the phantom foreign unionist menace, and concluded, "We won't just have a normal provincial election in B.C. We'll be carrying on a fight that will provide some direction to how the rest of the country is going to go."

Bennett dropped a few pre-election goodies, peekaboo glimpses of the budget that he wouldn't reveal. The next year's $500 million department of highways budget was introduced as a new job-creation program, and he suckered the Vancouver *Sun* into believing him. Great headline. He cooled out a blistering education scene with two deft moves. First, he unloaded Education Minister Bill Vander Zalm, whom he could never forgive for calling the Bennett government "gutless" and for drooling after Bennett's job. Vander Zalm would tell the world he jumped, he wasn't pushed. (Most people did believe that the ship was sinking, including Bennett's deputy, Norman Spector, who issued a confidential letter on the day the election campaign kicked off telling all deputy ministers they were entitled to a $100,000 severance package if they were fired.) Bennett made his second move once the election writ was dropped. Finding the cupboard not quite bare, he pumped another $45 million into education.

At a soggy Burnaby Chamber of Commerce lunch, Bennett told his audience, "We have to put our best face forward," and on Thursday, April 7, he called the election.

The business community reacted in its traditional non-partisan fashion. Stock hustler Peter Brown stopped collecting Socred campaign funds long enough to say that if the Socialist Hordes got back into power, he would move his Canarim Investment Corporation Ltd. operations to the free state of Alberta and added that mining and financial "activity in B.C. has virtually ceased until they see the outcome of the election." Construction giant H. Clark Bentall put all his Baptist zeal into a memo summoning the corporate tenants in the four massive office towers in the Bentall Centre in downtown Vancouver to a noon-hour Socred rally in Bentall Plaza. "This rally," he noted, "is to help in the re-election of our present government. It is most important that we have continued support for free enterprise, and this will be ensured by the return of Mr. Bennett and the Social Credit government."

This was the most centrally controlled, heavily monitored election campaign ever run in the province. At Socred Party headquarters, Jerry Lampert arranged for a Decima Research base camp for the duration. The first site, above Lampert's offices, was smoked out by intrepid reporters. The second, a mile away, was outfitted with twenty-seven phone lines. With them and the thirty-three lines already hooked up at Socred headquarters, Decima could make 4,500 two-minute calls per hour. The laboratory staff that created the Tough Guy was on full alert. Decima's Allan Gregg and Ian McKinnon would regularly plan strategy with Patrick Kinsella, Lampert, Bennett, and Doug Heal as data became available.

When the NDP came out of the gate, you would have thought they had already won the election. The Socred backroom boys had a few sleepless nights when they realized that both parties saw jobs as the key campaign issue. What gave them hope, however, was that Dave Barrett was

calling for a government public-works program, a rededica-
tion to Keynesian economic theory and government intervention – a return to the New Deal of an America clawing
its way out of the Dirty Thirties. Bill Bennett said governments don't create real jobs. Real jobs come from the private sector.

The NDP kept the Socreds on the run in the early days of
the campaign. As Barrett bounced through the NDP
heartland of Vancouver Island, it seemed that nothing
could go wrong. The NDP dredged up a document in the
bowels of the health ministry that promised increased user
fees for everything from visits to the doctor to restaurant
health inspections.

Bennett was caught off guard. With the riveting logic
that comes only to a politician during an election, Bill
Bennett told a luncheon gathering in Cranbrook that the
NDP's release of the health ministry document virtually
assured the re-election of a Social Credit government. "It
is," he argued, "a cheap and shoddy tactic to play upon the
fears of those people in order to divert attention from the
real issues in the campaign." With a Socred government
there would be no fee increases, now.

One week into the campaign, Bill Bennett hit bottom. As
he climbed on board his chartered plane after yet another
eighteen-hour day, he banged his head on the passageway
and practically stumbled to his seat. It was his birthday.
April 14. He was fifty-one years old.

The night before was his nomination meeting. He got a
cake, a pair of tennis shorts, and seamless adulation from a
standing-room-only crowd. That morning at 6.00 A.M. his
campaign bus had left Kelowna for the airport. Audrey was
with him, convinced by Kinsella that she could not avoid
the campaign. As Audrey and Bill stepped aboard the bus,
the press gang's answer to Hunter S. Thompson was in full
song: "Where is the fucking beer on this fucking bus?"

Bennett had the flu. On the plane ride to Terrace he tried
to snooze. He was on an uncertain journey to an NDP
stronghold that the technicians at Socred headquarters figured they could capture. Back on the ground, on his way to

the local radio station, a crowd of bellowing men, women, and children cornered Bennett near an alleyway. Before he could duck into the station doorway, a handful of eggs came flying through the air, spraying Bennett. After the broadcast he had to escape by ducking through a back door and down a side street.

It was dark by the time Bennett reached the Hudson Bay Lodge between Smithers and Terrace. Four hundred people had been waiting around for more than an hour. Just as he got to the stage, George Joseph, the hereditary chief of the Moricetown Band Reserve, started going at him. George was drunk, and Bennett was in trouble. George was strategically located in the middle of the room, and none of Bennett's handlers could get to him. For half an hour George raved on, mostly about the sellout to Alcan and its generating station at Kemano. Finally George slurred, "Bill, will you take me out for a beer? I'm broke."

Bennett reached in his pocket, pulled out a twenty, and handed it over, saying: "If that's all it takes, take your friend with you." The TV cameras caught it all. In the confusion that followed, Bennett cut his speech short and was led to the plane as the Northern Lights danced across the sky.

In the plane, he started to pace. And as he paced, he started to talk, first to no one in particular and then to Eli Sopow of the *Province* and Dan Smith of the *Toronto Star*. "The assholes," he muttered. "The assholes. I really don't need this." The man was a wreck. "I should just let the assholes have it." He slowly turned to Sopow and Smith. "This is the worst day in my life."

In Vancouver, an intelligence officer at the American Consulate was completing his confidential report for the State Department in Washington. It predicted an NDP win. Bennett, it said, had "lost touch" with the electorate; he "looks to be in trouble." And, it added, "We hear comments that the incumbent government is 'plastic' and operates by 'fiat out of an ivory tower'." The business community, "the mainstay of the Socred support", is "lukewarm". The report found that the provincial Liberals were "the

most interesting wild card"; there was a "distinct possibility" they would pick up a few seats. So much for
intelligence.

A week later Bennett still had the flu. On April 21, he and
Barrett were working the south-east corner of the province,
Bennett coming in as Barrett was leaving. The most recent
report from Socred pollsters was promising: the gap had
closed; the Socreds had pulled slightly ahead of the NDP.
Patrick Kinsella was travelling with Bennett, trying to pull
the show together; but Bennett was still floundering
around for an issue in a campaign that wasn't taking shape.
That morning he told an incredulous audience in Golden
that the greatest issue facing the people of British Columbia was the Crowsnest Pass freight rate, all because the
Socialist Hordes were in bed with their Liberal brothers and
sisters in Ottawa. Yawn.

Bennett's plan for the day was to proceed down the Columbia River Valley freshly paved with government hand-
outs: $800,000 for Golden, $40,000 for Canal flats, a
$460,000 forgivable loan for Invermere, the home town of
local candidate Jim Chabot.

As Bennett was heading south toward Cranbrook, Dave
Barrett's entourage was leaving the Cranbrook Town and
Country Motor Inn. His ancient DC-3, "Spirit of Cas-
ablanca", was off to Castlegar, where Fat Dave would belly
up to a huge breakfast at the Doukhobor Village. Day 14:
halfway through the campaign. On Dave's plate for the rest
of that day was the NDP's education policy, which he talked
about with CKQR open-line host Brian Pritchard for an easy
hour.

The early edition of the Vancouver *Sun* carried a relatively innocuous story, an interview with Barrett about the
Socred restraint program that would change the course of
the campaign. The lead – "A New Democratic Party government would not immediately dismantle the Social
Credit government's wage-restraint program" – was a bit
of a nothing. But it was enough of a scrap in the dog days of
mid-campaign for the assignment desk at BCTV to ask John
Gibbs, their man on the Barrett campaign, to get a follow-

up story. The opportunity presented itself at a scheduled press conference at 11:30 that morning at the Heritage Inn.

That's when Barrett blew away the NDP's chance of a victory. While the Vancouver *Sun* reporter sat amazed and the BCTV cameras rolled, Barrett blurted out: "The Rubber Room is dead. We would phase out the stabilization program as quickly as possible. It has a year to live. Until February. We would hope that before that time is up, Mr. Peck [the bureaucrat responsible for enforcing the program's guidelines] and his $300 a day [payment] could be handled in another way."

"So somebody in a union whose contract comes up between May 7, let's say, and next February, may find themselves under wage controls or may not?" asked Gibbs.

"They would not find themselves in any controls if the contracts were up after May 7 and the negotiations began then. However, anything before that time and up to that time . . . . We would have to go through each contractual obligation and go back over the process," Barrett replied.

"So zero to ten per cent is out as of May 7, if you are elected?" Gibbs asked, seeing a major story forming.

"The Rubber Room is out after May 7 to February next year." Barrett was adamant. "Those caught in the Rubber Room are going to have to be examined case by case. That is why there cannot be an overnight automatic termination of the stabilization plan."

This was all that was needed to confirm people's worst fears about the NDP: profligates shovelling money out of the back of the government truck, blowing a bundle on their friends in the trade-union movement while everyone else suffered. Proof that Barrett was everything the Socred machine made him out to be: a socialist hiding his red-underwear radical philosophy under a pinstriped suit of respectability. Until this press conference, all Barrett had said about restraint was warm porridge. Suddenly, for reasons he has yet to explain even to his closest friends, he took a hard line. You could hear the toilet flushing on Dave Barrett's political future.

Wayne Harding, Barrett's chief campaign cook and bottle washer, blanched. The blunder was obvious. As the *Sun* reporter headed for the phones to update his story, Harding called campaign headquarters in Vancouver with the bad news. So far Barrett had kept Bennett on the defensive, and the Socreds had stumbled over allegations of health-care cuts and union-bashing Labour Code amendments. Barrett was now on Bennett's turf.

While the BCTV tape was making its way to the coast on the regular run provided by the NDP, thank you very much, Bill Bennett's campaign bus was pulling away from a luncheon at Invermere. The BCTV reporter with that tour, Clem Chapple, had his own transportation and was taking a brief break, wandering about the sunny main street of town, when a young woman, a secretary from the town hall, came up to him: "Are you Clem Chapple? There's a phone call for you from Vancouver." It was his assignment editor with the news of the Barrett press conference. He had a high-tech possibility to blow the competition out of the water. BCTV's experimental mobile satellite happened to be heading toward Cranbrook, Bennett's evening destination. The plan was to go off the top of BCTV's "Newshour" with Barrett's statement and then go live to Bennett. On this one crucial evening, the dish would change the dynamic of the campaign in which, traditionally, one leader made a statement and it took a full twenty-four hours to get a response from his opponent, so that any sense of debate or attack was lost.

Chapple and his crew jumped into their car and sped off to catch up with Bennett, who was touring a sawmill at Canal Flats. It was 1:00 P.M. Chapple made the pitch to tour organizer Bud Smith. He told him Barrett planned to dump the restraint program, that BCTV had the tape. Bud used the two-way radio on the bus to check with the coast. By the time they reached the Town and Country Motor Inn in Cranbrook, the BCTV satellite was there, and the crew was stringing cables up the walls and through a window into Bennett's suite. Kinsella and Smith finally agreed to the broadcast, but they said Bennett had just taken a pill and was asleep. He hadn't been told what was happening.

As BCTV's "Newshour" went to air with an opening package on Barrett, the entire NDP campaign staff in Vancouver was glued to the tube. Barrett and Harding were watching in Nelson. Bill Bennett was just out of a shower and pulling on his shirt when Kinsella yelled into his bedroom: "Two minutes, boss." A slightly soggy, somewhat groggy Bill Bennett plopped down and had a microphone clipped on his open shirt, and Clem took it from there. "It was like handing the man a nuclear warhead and saying, 'Fire!' " Chapple recalls. Bennett put on his best performance of the campaign, as if he had Barrett by the throat. An hour later he met a standing-room-only crowd and poured it on with all the energy of a man who has been born again. There were tears in his eyes as he talked about his life in politics as service to the community. Pat Kinsella was on the sidelines bubbling to Chapple: "He's just thrown away the script." With seven days left to go, the Tough Guy was heading down the stretch.

When Barrett turned up at the NDP's election-planning committee meeting, his tongue was still in traction. He would spend the rest of the campaign trying to convince himself and anyone who would listen that the "Rubber Room" blunder didn't matter, but the canvassing results of NDP MLAs all over the province showed the centre fleeing to the right.

The Decima Research phone bank was just humming with good news. The Premier was told, don't talk. No matter what you're asked, don't say you will and don't say you won't. Just do what your dad used to do so well: just smile. And smile he did, as he peeled out of the back door of the Hotel Vancouver and headed east down Georgia for what his agenda described as a "one-hour walking tour of the Pacific Centre Mall".

The day was sunny. The time was just after noon. In one corner of the plaza the Socred brass band was playing "Happy Days Are Here Again". They were outfitted in matching blue-satin baseball jackets emblazoned with Premier Bill Bennett's name and a sun rising to orgasm across the back. At the centre of the mall a knot of people surrounded a four-fisted argument: one man was yelling about corrupt politicians and corrupt government; the other was yelling, "But, but, but." A group of Bennett boosters were forming up to one side: red sweat shirts, blue rugby pants, red and blue helium balloons, a clutch of hand-held campaign signs. Spontaneous. On the other side of the boiling mass was Peter Brown, the peripatetic Socred bagman: silk suit, suede Gucci loafers.

Nearby was Murray Pezzim, "The Pez", the Vancouver Stock Market prophet of penny possibilities, whose fortunes have been up and down so often he's installed an elevator in his stock portfolio. The Pez was clanging a brass bell and wearing a plastic boater and a blue T-shirt that read: "The Pez sez vote Socred."

The Pez stopped for a brief interview: "How much money has the street [the stock brokers on Howe Street] put into the Socred campaign?"

"More than $1 million," says the Pez, "and I'll tell you something. I've never seen the street get together on anything like this before."

One more question for the guru of gold mines while he waited for Bill, who was late. "Do you really think that if Fat Dave becomes premier he'll drive business away?"

"No way," says the Pez. "He's too smart a man for that."

It was then that the Pez spotted Bill Bennett coming full-tilt boogie with reporters in hot pursuit. When the Premier hit the plaza, he headed toward the indoor mall. In the lead were four cameramen attached by umbilical cords to their soundmen and all walking backwards recording this great event. On either side of this freight train of human movement there was a plainclothes cop with a bulge on his hip and a friendly but determined look in his eye. The reporters buzzed about like flies over warm meat. Mike Bailey, Bennett's traffic manager, took the point, searching for friendlies to meet his boss. And pulling up the rear were the two local candidates, the Premier's wife, Audrey, and the boys and girls in red and blue with colour co-ordinated balloons and signs.

In seven minutes and thirty seconds the entourage swarmed around the main level of the mall, down one escalator and up another; into a dress shop and out again; shake a hand and push a few aside. More voters are crushed than convinced. One man kept yelling, "Tell us the truth about Gracie's Finger, Bill," a reference to a bit of gerrymandering in Grace McCarthy's riding that Bill would rather forget. And every time Bill slowed down there were questions from reporters.

"What about education and health?" asked an intense young woman. As the answer arrived, her microphone cord was no longer connected to her tape recorder.

BCTV reporter Pamela Martin lunged in with, "Will you be raising taxes within the next nine months?" Nothing. She asked again, and again. Bill just grinned.

"Socreds suck," screamed an undecided voter.

"Go, Socreds, go," shouted a candidate and his son, trying to influence the undecided.

"Where are you getting all the extra money for the announcements you've been making this week, Mr. Bennett?" The question got lost in the jet stream as Mr. Bennett made an unexpected turn and leaped up another escalator. Then it was a dash to the doorway, zip down the street, and zap across the road into the safety of his bus, less than ten minutes after he arrived for a one-hour tour. And the band played on.

Election night at Bill Bennett's Kelowna headquarters was hot, sweaty, and jubilant. Bill finally entered, wearing his good-luck, light-brown suede jacket. He was beaming. The back-room pollsters would conclude that the winning issue was jobs; that the voters believed the Tough Guy when he said that private-sector jobs were more permanent and possible than the New Deal stuff Fat Dave was peddling.

None of that really mattered to Bennett. He believed that the people of British Columbia had voted for restraint. He had touched a nerve. He had a product that sold. Even though he gained only 1 per cent of the popular vote, making it 49 per cent Socred and 46 per cent NDP, his majority in the house was big enough – thirty-five seats to the NDP's twenty-two – to claim a "strong and enduring mandate". In the name of that mandate and his absolute fixation on restraint he would bring about the most radical revolution in B.C.'s history.

7

THE TIE THAT BINDS

In the Socred euphoria that followed the May 5 election, many in Bill Bennett's cabinet thought it would be business as usual. The messianic fervour that consumed the Tough Guy was not generally shared by his colleagues. The first cabinet meeting of the new government had little more on its agenda than getting out the budget; there was, after all, nothing clearly promised on the campaign trail except more of the same. Some energetic ministers in that meeting advanced the remnant of a pre-election plan, called Operation Homerun, developed by a handful of cabinet ministers and willing senior bureaucrats. The hit list included everything that rubbed these guys the wrong way about government, particularly teachers and their union, the education system, rent controls, and human-rights legislation.

Kinsella and Bennett had their own specific goals. The first was to make it clear to cabinet just who was boss. The second was to take advantage of a battered Opposition and a clear majority in the house to deal with some lingering frustrations.

This election victory was more than just the third win in a row for the Nouveau Socreds. For years Bennett's power in cabinet had been drifting and uncertain. In 1975 he had been beholden to "B.C.'s Number One Freedom Fighter", Grace McCarthy, for her legendary if overstated role in rebuilding the party and helping to free the province from the slavery of socialism. He also owed debts to the Liberal ship jumpers who had joined him in coalition. During his first term he was uncomfortable, awkward, and indecisive in government. The 1979 victory, a squeaker, was followed by scandals about everything from dirty election tricks to charges of interfering with the Electoral Reform Commission: gerrymandering, Gracie's Finger. Bennett spent most of that term playing hide-and-seek with the press and fending off challengers for his throne. Then he found Restraint, and Pat Kinsella found the Tough Guy. Restraint and the Tough Guy won the 1983 election. The party, the cabinet, the backbenchers had just been along for the ride. It was time to make that point.

Bennett's first move was to dump Gracie as deputy premier. Thereafter, every order-in-council would be signed by none other than Bill Bennett. He was in absolute command.

The agenda of this new era of one-man rule was hammered out in the heat of the Okanagan summer at Lake Okanagan Resort, a rambling, Spanish-style stucco retreat of private condominiums, tennis courts, and public meeting rooms that had fallen into receivership. Don't forget your tennis shorts.

Michael Walker, the Fraser Institute's tall, balding youthful-yet-portly high priest was the perfect choice as after-dinner faith healer in the Socred tent. He is Adam Smith's "invisible hand" of the marketplace come to live among us. In 1973, when monied folk in the B.C. mining community were introducing Bill Bennett to Marty Goldfarb and plotting to get rid of the NDP, young Michael was an unhappy economist working in the ivory tower of the federal finance department's policy-development branch. This son of a Newfoundland miner picked up his Ph.D. from the University of Western Ontario and became disillusioned teaching the *de rigueur* economic theory of the day: economic models can be built to predict the future. He developed a passion for monetarism, the new doctrine advanced by American economist Milton Friedman, which became the essence of Reaganomics. (Over the years Walker's bond with Friedman went beyond an economic philosophy. The men shared an interest in racket sports and woodworking and, as Walker observed, "He's bald and I'm bald.") Walker worked for the Bank of Canada and was the first to argue to the governor that the bank should adopt a monetarist strategy.

In the fall of 1973, Walker received a phone call from his old roommate at Western, Csaba Hajdu, an economist with MacMillan Bloedel. Hajdu's boss, Pat Boyle, like the corporate executives who were bankrolling Goldfarb, was interested in developing a little intellectual ammunition to knock Barrett out of the box. Hajdu talked about it to Walker.

In the spring of 1974 Walker was joined at Finance by Ed Clark, father of the National Energy Program. One more reason for Walker to leave. Walker flew out to meet Pat Boyle, Hajdu's boss at MacBlo, who convinced Walker that his work would be more than simply getting rid of the socialists in Victoria; it would be "non-partisan". (In B.C. "non-partisan" still meant getting rid of the socialists.) He would deal with ideas not politics. This appealed to Walker, who advanced the notion that "if you really want to change the world you have to change the . . . ideological fabric of the world." Boyle offered "a modest amount" of seed money, and the business community guaranteed a loan for $200,000. The Fraser Institute was born in November 1974.

A decade later the institute operates on a $900,000 annual budget and shines its guiding light across continents. Michael Walker frequently consults with governments and their commissions, charging no fee but expenses, and has dispensed his increasingly popular view of economic salvation to virtually all governments in Canada except that socialist lot running Manitoba.

Fraser Institute authors include Milton Friedman and Simon Fraser University's Herbert Grubel, who theorizes that unemployment-insurance schemes create more unemployment and social programs to help single mothers create more single mothers. (He has yet to tackle whether an expanding funeral industry leads to increased mortality rates.) Institute publications sell worldwide and have made their way onto the required reading lists at Harvard, MIT, UCLA, the University of Victoria, and Memorial University of Newfoundland, among others. The editorial board includes a couple of Nobel laureates and Sir Alan Walters, Margaret Thatcher's personal economic guru. William F. Buckley, Jr., brother-in-law of Socred bagman Austin Taylor, Jr., is a favourite guest speaker. (The institute displays an odd zealousness about media coverage. The annual report observed that Michael Walker preached the institute's message in 230 media interviews in 1983 alone. Reviews of institute books were carried in such diverse publications as the *Calvinist Contact*, the Halifax *Chronicle-Herald*, and the *Toronto Star*.)

Among the institute's many activities is the Centre for the Study of Economics and Religion, headed up by Walter Block, the institute's chief economist. Walter goes about lecturing to theological groups on subjects such as: "There is nothing immoral about the honest quest for profits." When the Canadian Catholic Bishops delivered a body blow to the capitalist system because of its lack of concern for the unemployed, Walter Block delivered a body blow to the Canadian Bishops. On born-again Christian Jimmy Pattison's Vancouver radio station CJOR one bright morning, Walter advanced the free-market-fundamentalist theory that the Canadian Red Cross could overcome its chronic shortage of blood by ending voluntary donations and buying and selling the stuff.

The institute's board of directors includes representatives from major Canadian and international mining and forestry corporations, a glittery list of executives in finance, manufacturing, and communications – from Sam Belzberg at First City Trust, and Sonja Bata of Bata Limited to A.J. deGrandpré at Bell Canada and Lorne Lodge, chief executive officer at IBM Canada. The institute supplements its budget deficits through modest membership fees and the sales of Poleconomy, a board game invented by a New Zealand dishwasher that tests political and financial instincts. (It also picks up some spare change flogging "Adam

Smith" silk ties. Owners include Ronald Reagan, Bill Bennett, Michael Walker, and Milton Friedman. This is the tie that binds.)

It has been a long but rewarding ministry for Walker and the institute. Their network is international; their influence is considerable and growing. British Columbia is a beacon to the world, a mission station for evangelists of the new right. What Patrick Kinsella and the Baby Blue Machine brought to Socred politics, the Fraser Institute will bring to Socred economic policy. "I think the way policy gets changed," says Walker, "is by creating an ethos in which politicians will see it is in their interest to make those kinds of choices."

That ethos is palpable as the Okanagan evening air begins to cool and Walker heads into the main meeting area. After the breaking of bread he sets about his sermon. He insists that B.C. is not experiencing a normal cyclical slump in resource revenues. The balloon has burst. For several years Socred budgets have been fuelled by natural gas revenues. (When Dave Barrett was premier he put the arm on Ottawa and the National Energy Board to allow B.C. to increase the export price of natural gas. Then he set up the B.C. Petroleum Corporation to siphon off the increased royalties into the B.C. treasury. Billy and the Socreds went through that extra cash like a Kelowna Coke float.) As Walker puts it: "The royalty revenue in natural gas . . . is what allowed the government to ignore the emerging fiscal reality as they framed their expenditure program through the later part of the 1970s."

The Socreds, according to Walker, "were not behaving like a government that understood what the income realities were." He told them that, for the foreseeable future, their revenues from mining and forestry would not be great. There was no point trying to save or maintain existing social programs, for, "What they were looking at was not a temporary aberration." The revenue would simply not come back.

The second part of Walker's lesson moved from one area of government expenditure to another, from education to health care to social services. He preached the Fraser Institute's general dogma of cutbacks to social services and the introduction of user fees, plus a healthy dollop of deregulation and incentives to the private sector. But the most compelling part of Walker's message dealt with how to make these cuts. Walker borrowed from his soulmate, Milton Friedman, and from American neo-conservative social scientist Mancur Olson, author of *The Rise and Decline of Nations*, a tome that has been, of late, bedtime reading for Bennett's private think-tank, Norman Spector.

Friedman and Olson figure that a major problem threatening the free-enterprise system is "special-interest groups" that gum up the works. Doctors, lawyers, and trade unionists all control membership to their organizations to keep their incomes high. In Olson's words: "Special interest organizations and collusions reduce efficiency and aggregate income in the societies in which they operate and make political life more divisive." If governments are serious about cutting costs and getting free enterprise back up to speed, they have to break the grip of the special-interest groups that prey upon their budgets, sap the vital fluids of the marketplace, and create political turmoil with their lobbies and protests.

Special-interest groups would become central to Bill Bennett's thinking. He would single them out for attack as part of his strategy to keep the province polarized. They were "the coalition of dissent", a gang of incorrigible delinquents worthy of Bill Bennett's Tough Love. He labelled them "bad British Columbians", and described them as a disruptive evil force, as "the tyranny of the minority" standing in the way of economic salvation.

At eleven o'clock, after spreading the good news, Michael Walker was shown to one of the condominiums, where he caught a few hours' sleep. By six the next morning, just as Bill Bennett, Pat McGeer, and a couple of the other lads in the cabinet were pulling on their tennis whites for an invigorating hour of doubles, Michael Walker began the long bumpy ride to Kelowna, the airport, and the coast. The return flight would bring the deputy ministers, with their tennis rackets and briefing books, to face the new reality and the Tough Guy transcendent.

By now Patrick Kinsella was easing up on the job. "The name of the game," he was fond of saying, "is to win." He had won. Time to look for a new game. He sat quietly on a hill above the courts, in a pastel T-shirt from his Lacoste collection and summer slacks. (A bit of vanity. He once strolled on board an Air B.C. seaplane from Victoria to Vancouver dressed entirely in pink: pink jacket, pink tie, pink shirt, pink slacks, pink socks, and pink shoes.) Below him and a few yards to his right was Bill Bennett at his game, fanatically fit, relentlessly aggressive. But Kinsella's mind was in the East on the federal Tory leadership. He was planning to set up a consulting firm to convert his growing political clout into profit. He was waiting to hear if his old boss, Bill Davis, was going to pull the plug in Ontario and go after Joe Clark. If he didn't, Kinsella would work for his friend Michael Wilson and ultimately convince Wilson to go to Brian Mulroney. Anyone but Clark.

All in good time. For now, breakfast; then meetings with deputies still stunned by the Socred victory and ministers just beginning to learn who was boss. The meeting rooms were crowded, dimly lit, and cool. The tables were stacked with thick briefing books to assist the politicians and their bureaucrats to attack or defend sacred cows. Ministry by ministry the tough budget items were presented.

The session was a bit like the Schooner Cove retreat that had developed the first restraint program. There was the usual range from the talented insightful people to the bull-shitters more interested in covering their backs with white noise. But, in the end, six basic themes were developed on which to build a budget and redefine the social contract of British Columbia.

"User-pay" topped the list. During the previous two years, the Socreds had tended toward fees and away from taxes to generate revenue. For the first time since Wacky Bennett refined the province's medicare program and reduced the cost of a hospital stay to $1 a day, that principle of a token payment was tossed out and the fee was tripled. The government now asked if there was any "socially redeeming" reason for subsidizing services that may be "desirable" but not necessarily "essential".

Deregulation was pursued with equal vigour, to reduce the cost of government by removing expensive bureaucracies that mediated and regulated. The Rentalsman's service was the most prominent target. Getting rid of the Rentalsman was not removing power from tenants or landlords; it returned freedom and decision making to individuals. The Rentalsman's powers and staff were a government bureaucracy that encouraged disputes by funding a venue for them. The Socred cabinet and their advisers argued that if you got rid of the Rentalsman, landlords and tenants would have to come together in a spirit of cooperation and work out their differences. Ah, the simplicity of a bygone era. They could also clog the courts and pay small fortunes for lawyers, but the government's legal apparatus was not included in the cost estimates.

The thinking on "pass-through costs" proved the most intriguing. Between 50 and 60 per cent of the construction industry in B.C. was funded by government in some way. Virtually all that work was performed by unionized contractors and union workers. When the unionized construction industry signed a new agreement with the B.C. and Yukon Territory Building and Construction Trades Council, the costs were passed through to the government. The government had no say in the negotiations, but the unions had a lock on major projects: so the costs of everything from schools and hospitals to ports and roads were high. This captive marketplace is one that Mancur Olson delights in criticizing. The problem, he argued, and the Socreds agreed, is that the unions haven't enough competition. The free market can't work when some jurisdictions, like municipalities or school districts, restrict bids on construction projects to union firms.

Over lunch, ministers and their deputies pondered the free market and then went for a stretch in the sunshine. Amid the Bermuda shorts, knobby knees, and toasted noses of the two dozen or so power brokers, there were three women. Consumer and Corporate Affairs deputy minister Jill Bodkin, who survived the spending scandal that nailed her boss, Peter Hyndman, joined Ministry of Labour acting deputy minister Isabel Kelly, who was responsible for women's programs. Both wore cotton skirts and short-sleeved blouses. The third was former deputy premier Grace McCarthy, the Minister of Welfare, resplendent in her finest white blouse and harem pants set off by white and gold accessories, carrot-red hair, and pearl-encrusted sandals.

At a circular table near the pool an industrious cameraman was setting up his gear. Before the cue was given to roll, Bennett carefully removed a beer bottle from the camera's sight line. Ever vigilant. Then he spoke. The deficit he refused to discuss during the election campaign, the deficit for the budget he refused to introduce, would not be between $600 million and $900 million as speculated in the morning paper. Those figures "are not only low, not only way low, they are way, way, way, way low." Why this sudden zeal to emphasize the negative? All the better to justify tax increases, drastic cuts in social services, and further limiting of public-sector wage increases. Softening up the body politic.

Back at the conference table, privatization was up for discussion. Rendering unto the private sector has been Bill Bennett's goal ever since he created BCRIC and convinced thousands of people to pay $6 a share for assets they already owned. The finance ministry would argue that turning government functions over to the private sector makes good economic sense. Governments make lousy pricing decisions: not because they are a monopoly and not because they are inefficient managers. The problem is the political pressure to underprice services through "invisible subsidies".

This is the next step in the user-pay argument. Although there is no guarantee that the private sector will perform the service for less money, there is a guarantee that there will be fewer people on the public payroll. Privatization is part of "downsizing".

It is also politically astute. Rod Dobell, the head of the University of Victoria's School of Public Administration, put it most succinctly: when you move a service from the public sector to the private sector, you create "jobs for the boys". You make work for people who believe in what you do and who will most likely vote for you. You take work from people who are public-sector union members and less likely to want you to be the government.

There were two more items on the agenda: automation (can computers replace people to save money or allow the government to "downsize" the public service) and wages – public-service wages and the Compensation Stabilization Program. It became clear that the CSP promised for a two-year term in February '82, would be extended indefinitely. To enforce the CSP, the government would have to tighten its grip on tax sources and budgets for schools, hospitals, and municipalities. Independent boards and commissions would have to have their powers clipped. Restraint meant not only redistributing money to the private sector; it meant redistributing power from "special-interest groups" to the hands of a central government.

As the meeting at Lake Okanagan Resort came to an end, Bill Bennett was feeling smug. His decision, made with Patrick Kinsella, to go into the election without a budget in place and to run a campaign filled with vague suggestions to stay the course had worked like a charm. That evening the chatter on the courts was all of a task practically accomplished. The budget could be reworked and ready to roll within a month. The legislation would be drafted and printed by early July. The legislative session would be a snap. By the August long weekend, at the latest, everyone could be playing tennis full-time.

8

TOUGH LOVE

Swollen with anticipation of real news – as always at budget time – the press corps is herded into the ballroom at the Harbour Towers Hotel in Victoria, on the morning of July 7, 1983. At the budget lockup sandwiches appear – chopped egg, salmon, and ham – neatly quartered on white and brown, garnished with black pitted olives and sweet mixed pickles. Lots of coffee. Government officials are presented to answer questions, off the record, long before you are ready for them, as always. Just before you stumble on to what you think is the key that will unlock the mysteries of the government's fiscal philosophy, the officials disappear. The sandwiches also disappear, brown bread first, as always.

Two weeks earlier the Throne Speech, the traditional introduction to the budget, contained the usual collection of hopes for the future and reminiscences of visitors or regrets for those who had passed on after serving the people of the province. There was a note about the visit by Her Majesty, Queen Elizabeth II, and the passing of former MLA Mrs. Isabel Dawson, Shirley Owen, the widow of the late lieutenant-governor, Walter Owen, and a few others. There was the usual uplifting note: "As we begin to emerge from the winter of our adversity. . . . Rather than sinking into despondency and pessimism, our people are demonstrating pride, resilience and strength" – a fragile recovery worth nurturing. There were some nice words about "a mandate to improve our industrial relations", and a promise to "pursue job creation in the public sector".

Then in a few brief paragraphs, there were unusual intimations of a fundamental change in government, more than a nip here and a tuck there to save a few bucks. Distant cannon were sounding faintly. Election rhetoric on the popular theme of pillorying a greedy, complacent public service was there in spades. It suggested that they achieved their luxurious life at the expense of the private sector, indifferent to the private sector's plight. The polarization that precedes a Bennett attack was strategically activated:

> . . . many of those working in the private sector have been subject to marketplace controls – bankruptcies, unemployment, layoffs, low or non-existent wage increases – and in many cases actual decreases. . . . On the other hand, those working in the public sector largely have been sheltered from the impact of the recession. While wage increases have moderated, it is evident that taxpayers and the unemployed can no longer support the level of public services, including attendant employment levels, that have grown up in the past thirty years.

Bill Bennett neglected to point out that the target of this crusade was a government developed and expanded in all but three of the past thirty years by Wacky and Billy. Without a blush, the born-again Bennett gave a testimonial of his new-found faith, attacking his own government's policies.

> My government has given careful attention to the successive layers of agencies, boards and commissions that have grown up around government within the last fifteen years. Measures will be introduced to streamline the operations of some of these bodies, eliminate those whose functions have become unnecessary in light of market conditions, better define the respective responsibilities of agencies and the courts, and introduce restraint measures where such bodies continue to exist.

Radical stuff. And there was more. "My government believes that an intrusive and overweight public sector – far from being part of the solution to our economic difficulties – is in fact part of the problem." Along with the plan to reduce the size of the public service, this bit of curious logic was offered: "Individual public servants will be expected to do more with less, but strong efforts will be made to simplify procedures and eliminate obstacles to higher productivity. The result should be a greater level of job satisfaction as well as improved service to the public."

Art Kube, the new boy at the head of the B.C. Federation of Labour, had that throne speech still bouncing about his cranium when he recalled a meeting he had on a Vancouver-bound ferry a few days after the election. As the vessel pulled out of Swartz Bay and threaded its way toward Active Pass, Kube bumped into an old acquaintance, Ian McKinnon, the other half of Decima Research. Kube wondered out loud just what Bill Bennett had in mind for his new term in office and concluded from his talk with the man's pollster that the election rhetoric would fade and calm would return to the land. After all, hadn't provincial secretary Jim Chabot sent out a memo in January to all the government workers to dampen the rumours about civil-service cuts? The little pay-packet missive reassured more than 40,000 workers that the government "does not wish to take abrupt action in reducing the size of the public service. Massive layoffs are not desirable. The government objective – and my personal objective – is to avoid layoffs and minimize the disruptions to government workers and to the public alike."

Any revolution still seemed distant to reporters reading the budget that Thursday morning. There were the cuts that everyone expected: "budgetary adjustments", as the minister of finance put it, "to reflect reduction or elimination of regional offices in the ministries of forests, provincial secretary and government services, environment, finance, municipal affairs, transportation and highways, consumer and corporate affairs, and lands, parks and housing." It was all very clinical. No people were involved, just "offices". And there was nothing in the budget figures to suggest that anything would be wiped out.

A few long-time Socred enemies were fiscally man-handled. The Agricultural Land Commission was clipped by 37 per cent. The Human Rights operation was reduced by 22 per cent. Money was tweaked from women's programs. The ministry of labour's employment-training program would operate with $10 million dollars less, even though the throne speech had promised increased attention to job creation. Student aid would shrink. Special-education programs were about 12 per cent less special than the year before. Forestry programs in silviculture, harvesting, research, and forest protection got trimmed. And the Rentalsman, the Auditor General, and the Ombudsman would all be squeezed. But only squeezed.

There was only one glaring tax hike: sales tax was increased one point to 7 per cent, and for the first time tax would be charged on restaurant meals and long-distance telephone calls. Everything else was fairly consistent. It was the lean mean lingo of the Fraser Institute. Privatization and some incentives to small business.

A few niggling points. It looked as if the government was getting rid of some land holdings adjacent to Tranquille, an institution for the severely mentally and physically handicapped at Kamloops. Question to the government experts: Does this mean the government is getting rid of Tranquille and moving those people somewhere else? Answer: No.

Just how and when all this "downsizing" would come about was not clear. From the budget all you could glean was a line about "initiatives affecting" a variety of government operations including the Rentalsman and the Human Rights Commission. But there was still money in the budget, so one could assume nothing would be immediate.

The whole thing seemed simple enough: Bill Bennett stays the restraint course and kicks business in the teeth with a sales-tax hike. Spending is up over 12 per cent; another inflationary budget. Most scribes stop their scribbling long before the lockup is lifted at 14:30 hours, when the finance minister stands to read his budget speech to the

Solidarity Coalition's leaders, Father Jim Roberts and
Renate Shearer.

Bill and Wacky after Bill's first election victory in 1975:
"a kind of psychic patricide."

Jimmy Pattison — "There is no limit to what a man can do or where he can go if he doesn't mind who gets the credit."

Patrick Kinsella, the self-confessed "best political hack in the country."

Bill Bennett in "election mode" 1983.

Bill Bennett putting his "best face forward."

Art Kube: down and out at home in his Dior velour robe, waiting for Jack Munro's phone call from Kelowna.

Confirming the latest Expo 86 estimated deficit at $311 million: (l to r) Peter (Petesy) Brown, Jimmy Pattison and Michael Bartlett.

Vancouver Province

Roy Gauthier addressing a crowd of angry trade unionists protesting the use of non-union labour at the
Pennyfarthing site, 1984.

Running for re-election 1983: The 7½ minute dash through the Pacific Centre Mall.

Solidarity Rally Empire Stadium, August 10, 1983:
When the Firemen's band came in and marched around
the track, people actually had tears in their eyes.

B.C. Fed. vice-president Jack Munro who discovered, to his astonishment, that the trade unionists were the "moderates" in Solidarity.

Dave Barrett's last hurrah: the 1983 campaign.

Announcing the BCGEU settlement, Sunday November 13, 1983: (l to r) Norman Spector, Vince Ready and Cliff Andstein.

Solidarity in the streets: 50,000 people march on the
Socred Convention, October 15, 1983.

The Socialist Hordes are at the gates — of the Hotel Vancouver. Inside, celebrating Socreds cheer Bennett's declaration that, "We will not back down on what we set out to do."

legislature. The press shuffles back to the legislative buildings hauling their electronic gear. Phone calls are made to
various assignment editors. No sweat, boss, it's in the bag.
We'll ship everything over as soon as the minister finishes
his budget and holds his press conference.

And then it hits. There are usually one or two pieces of
innocuous enabling legislation, and everyone expected one
to change the sales tax and another to allow interim spending while the budget was being debated. Instead, minister
after minister rises with rehearsed precision and introduces
bill after bill after bill. The Opposition is caught in the
blizzard. At first Barrett leisurely leans over to pick up the
newest piece of legislation from the clerk's desk and pass it
to the appropriate critic. Then the snowball picks up speed;
the NDP tries to contain the Socred avalanche, but finally,
they are buried by it. Journalists flee first to the phones to
warn their bosses that all is not as usual. Then they flood
into the press-gallery lounge to intercept blue-jacketed sergeants ascending the narrow gallery stairway loaded down
with copies of bills. It is like a Boxing Day sale as reporters
lunge to grab the latest piece of legislation. A reporter with
the bills piled up in his lap is yelling: "Good Lord, they've
dumped the Human Rights Commission." Then another
scribe: "The Rentalsman is gone. Rent controls are gone.
Tenants can be evicted without cause." And another:
"School boards are losing control of their budgets. Regional
districts have lost their power to plan." Then the first
fellow again: "Look at this. Just look at this. They're going
to fire public servants without cause. I can't believe it." A
sneak attack. A predawn raid. A complete surprise.

It takes only a few days to sweep through the legislation,
sniff out the finer points, and discover where the mines are
buried.

Bill 2: The Public Service Labour Relations Amendment
Act is a clumsy bit of surgery that guts the Government
Employees' Union collective agreement, leaving the BCGEU
to negotiate nothing but wages, which are already strictly
controlled by the Compensation Stabilization Act and its
regulations.

Bill 3: The Public Sector Restraint Act puts 200,000 provincial public servants on notice that they can be terminated without cause once their current collective agreements expire. The major contract with the BCGEU expires October 31, 1983. There may be compensation, but you can kiss your seniority protection goodbye.

Bill 4: The Income Tax Amendment Act removes two tax credits for poor people – tenants and the elderly – that had been introduced by the Socreds to help these people deal with some particularly stiff tax increases the general public was facing.

Bill 5: The Residential Tenancy Act gets rid of the Rentalsman and his mediation service as of September 30, 1984. Rent controls are abolished. If you and your landlord end up at each other's throats you can tell it to the judge, but you may not want to risk it: landlords can evict their tenants without cause.

Bill 6: The Education (Interim) Finance Act removes all budget-making power from school boards and places it in the hands of the minister of education. Centralization of power in the name of restraint emerges as a major theme.

Bill 9: The Municipal Amendment Act removes zoning authority from regional districts. This bill is dubbed the "Spetifore Amendment", in honour of George Spetifore, a potato farmer and contributor to the campaign chest of Walter Davidson, speaker of the house and MLA from Delta. Spetifore argued that he should be able to grow buildings on his land instead of spuds. The municipality of Delta liked the idea of taking the farm land out of the Agricultural Land Reserve; but the plan was stopped by "a socialist-communist conspiracy", Davidson's soubriquet for the Lower Mainland Regional District. Spetifore sold the land to a consortium headed by a car-dealer buddy of Davidson's. This new legislation was going to make buildings grow.

Bill 11: The Compensation Stabilization Amendment Act lifts the two-year sunset clause on wage controls and extends it indefinitely. As well, public-sector wages can be rolled back.

Bill 19: The Institute of Technology Amendment Act gives the minister of education control over what courses and programs will be offered or cancelled at the B.C. Institute of Technology. It also rejigs the method of appointments and the makeup of the board of governors. Faculty, staff, and student representation on the board are eliminated.

Bill 20: The College and Institute Act is like Bill 19. The government can call the shots on courses and board membership. Representation on college boards from locally elected school boards is terminated; so are three advisory councils on course development that involved members of the community: the Occupational Training Council, the Academic Council, and the Management Advisory Council.

Bill 21: The Crown Corporations Reporting Repeal Act gets rid of a legislative committee that Bennett boasted about setting up shortly after he beat the socialists in 1975. The committee became a bit of an embarrassment as it delved into the peculiar goings on at various Crown corporations. The committee's research staff of five join the unemployment line.

Bill 23: The Motor Vehicle Amendment Act eliminates government-owned vehicle-testing stations. Annual vehicle tests are no longer required. The inspectors are fired.

Bill 24: The Medical Services Act concentrates power in Victoria to dictate where in the province new doctors can practise if they want to collect their fees from the government medicare scheme. Also, opting out of medicare is an easier choice for doctors.

Bill 26: The Employment Standards Amendment Act is another swipe at workers' power. Employer liability for back wages in a bankruptcy is reduced. The Employment Standards Board is wiped out. If you have a problem you can go to court. It also takes the province-wide bottom line out of labour standards. Contracts can be negotiated for working conditions below the provincially set levels.

Bill 27: The Human Rights Act. The minister of labour insists that "When the smoke clears this will be the best piece of human rights legislation in the country." It wipes out the Human Rights Branch and the independent Human Rights Commission and replaces them with a government-appointed council with no fixed term.

"Mental and physical handicaps" are added to the specific grounds for discrimination, but this actually limits the rights of the disabled, who have been covered under a broader clause prohibiting "discrimination without reasonable cause". That clause has been deleted, opening up the possibility of discrimination against, for example, pregnant women or homosexuals. Both the minister and the council are given more arbitrary power in pursuing discrimination complaints.

The old legislation made it illegal to publish a discriminatory employment advertisement or to require an applicant to furnish information on race, religion, or political beliefs. That section was deleted. A complainant now must prove "intent" to discriminate. A guilty party can no longer be fined for damages. The government is no longer a party to complaints, so complainants must provide a lawyer, witnesses, and other evidence. If you don't like the way you're being treated when you lodge a complaint you can no longer go to the Ombudsman; the minister has been given the power to show him the door.

At 16:10 hours on July 7, Human Rights Branch director Hanne Jensen was handed the legislation that made her job redundant before being hauled into a meeting with three of her superiors. She emerged at 17:30 hours ashen and badly shaken: they were firing her staff out from under her. When the smoke did indeed clear, the director of the Human Rights Branch, the commissioners, and virtually all the staff had been terminated in the seven offices around the province.

In the countryside, senior civil servants had been dispatched before noon on July 7 and were waiting to strike on command. Stuart Goodings, an assistant deputy minister in Consumer and Corporate Affairs, hit the government's consumer centre on Hornby Street at 15:30 hours and blew away twenty-four workers. They were fired, redundant. A total of four more were nailed in Prince George, Kamloops, and Victoria. Funding for consumer services was slashed; funding for private consumer groups was discontinued.

A man walked into the government motor vehicle testing station in Nanaimo. He introduced himself as a ministry employee and instructed the supervisor, Al Edwards, to terminate his eight staff members. Then he terminated Al Edwards.

At 18:30 hours nine field officers and five secretaries were terminated at the recreation and sports branch in Nanaimo. Jim Patterson, the Rentalsman, was summoned back from leave in Europe. He reached his office at 14:00 hours and dropped the axe on most of his senior staff at 15:00 hours: they had until the end of September to rearrange their lives. They got the news in the new boardroom in the new facility the operation had moved into one week earlier.

In the midst of the action a telex was released from the provincial secretary, Jim Chabot: "We are firm in our resolve to reduce the size and cost of government, but we intend to be fair and sensitive in our implementation plans."

There was no pattern to the firing. Seniority was not a factor. Mary Jahraus was a receptionist/librarian with six years seniority; her husband drove a cab. Frank Whiteley worked for the Rentalsman. He had twenty-three years government seniority. He was in his sixties. His wife didn't work. Terri Bernardet was a consumer services clerk with eight years seniority; she is a mother of three; her husband was unemployed.

Bill Bennett's summer offensive was perfectly timed. The Tough Guy had talked with his pollsters and exposed his politically sensitive gut to the prevailing breezes: he knew the mood of the province was not charitable. Most people saw no salvation in John Maynard Keynes, who had inspired massive government spending on public projects and well-maintained social safety nets, first in Sweden and then in North America. A political solution based on a

1930s gospel, goosed by the brotherly love of the '60s, was not selling. Government was no longer the solution; it was part of the problem.

The pollsters who regularly test the heartbeat of the nation whispered one consistent message. The recession of 1981-82 had forced people to re-evaluate their attitudes. The recession hit harder in Canada than in the U.S.A., and harder on the coast than in the centre of the country. Canadian savings rates were twice those south of the border and double the level of a decade ago. People were starting to pay off their long-term debts. In the parlance of the pollsters, middle-and upper-middle-class wage earners were becoming much more "risk aversive". This was not a confident time.

There was a growing fear of unemployment. People knew people who were having trouble finding jobs for the first time in their lives. Well-trained people were out of work; university graduates were out of work. Attitudes toward trade unions were hardening; public-sector unionists, who had both job security and the right to strike, were particularly unpopular.

It was all in the throne speech.

The prejudices that slumber beneath the surface of every society were being awakened by the deafening recession. If Bill Bennett did nothing else with his budget and the stack of legislation that went along with it, he made people feel comfortable with those prejudices. Marty Goldfarb explained the appeal of Bill Bennett's revolution: "I see him acting out what people would like to see acted out at a political level. I see him doing it in a crass way because he is not very sophisticated; but I see him doing what the average guy would do if you put him in his position."

It was also the right time of year for the Tough Guy's offensive. It was summer. Most of the body politic was at the beach. More importantly, teachers were at the cottage, travelling, dispersed. The teachers had been trouble for every B.C. government for fifteen years. They are credited with toppling Wacky. They abandoned the NDP when Barrett terrorized the education system in his own way. Their leadership was becoming increasingly militant as they saw what Bennett's restraint program would do to the school system and their job security.

With teachers out of the way for a while, Bill Bennett could seize new objectives. The other forces that had once hindered his advance were nowhere to be found in July 1983. The NDP were dead in the water. No one would suggest the Opposition had ever been a major influence on Bennett's style of government; but on the odd occasion when he convened the legislature and allowed debate, there had been some pressure to moderate. There had been at least some prospect that the leader of the Opposition would catch the public imagination and unseat the government. In 1983, however, there was no leader of the Opposition save one fat, lame duck.

Barrett had announced he was leaving. He was drained of energy, bereft of ideas; his battered caucus were in no mood for a long legislative session. They were preoccupied with replacing Fat Dave, and had been jockeying openly from the moment the election results were final. A budget, a few bits of legislation, a pinch of salt rubbed into their wounds, and then they could get on to the real business at hand.

The second force was the B.C. Federation of Labour, arguably the most highly organized, well-financed, militant force of its kind in North America. But Jim Kinnaird, their fire-breathing leader, had dropped dead two months before Bill Bennett kicked off his campaign; and no leader had been found until June. Even then it was a reluctant choice: Art Kube, a chain-smoking, lumbering bureaucrat.

For a time Kube had worked as the B.C. educational director for the Canadian Labour Congress. He was not, like the other BCFed executives, a leader or former leader of a union; he was not known as a labour spokesman. His speaking was hindered by a discernible Polish accent, a tendency to turn an academic phrase, and a monotonous voice. He was more comfortable twisting delegates' arms at the back of a convention hall than he would ever be giving tub-thumping speeches to the masses.

Kube's appointment was typical of the fights and splits that have dominated BCFed politics since the cold-war days of the 1950s, when the forces on the right, who would come to be identified as social democrats, tried to drive the communists and radicals out of the leadership of the trade-union movement. When they failed, they drove the communist-led unions out of the BCFed. Back in those days Art Kube was a commie-basher. Now he had become the president of the BCFed because the big unions, including BCGEU and the IWA, wanted to block the left-wing candidate, Leif Hansen of the meatcutters' local of the United Food and Commercial Workers.

The effects of Kube's inexperience and the lukewarm and wavering support of his executive were aggravated by two factors. Relations with the Social Credit government had been on a war footing for all of Bill Bennett's time in power. Except for occasional chats between IWA head Jack Munro and Bill Bennett, public scrapping and lobbying had been done through the NDP. Organized labour was best at cutting a better deal for its members, and it really didn't give a damn about its public image. Bill Bennett liked it that way. When Kube came to office, the NDP had no leader and no clear agenda. Kube and the BCFed would be on their own.

The balance of power was shifting within the BCFed, not just from left to right but from private-sector, male-dominated, blue-collar unions to public-sector, white-collar unions in which the vast majority of members were women. Bill Bennett was quick to capitalize on the fact that the recession was undermining B.C.'s resource base in mining and forestry and devastating private-sector union ranks while leaving the public sector relatively unscathed. The IWA, once the biggest union in the province, dropped from 40,000 to 26,000 members in two years and was easily eclipsed by the B.C. Government Employees' Union. That shift in power also meant a shift in the issues. The trade-union movement was being called on to move beyond the traditional bread-and-butter stuff to less clearly defined issues of social justice: human rights, equal pay, and daycare.

Finally, there was the Employers' Council of British Columbia, a traditional ally of Bill Bennett's government, although during the decade Bill Hamilton was president there was some friction. Hamilton maintained what most people considered an independent and humane, if right-wing, view. He stepped down virtually on the eve of the July 7 budget to join the Macdonald Commission on the economy. His replacement, Jim Matkin, was a gift to Bill Bennett.

Matkin, the man with the Harvard law degree, spent his undergraduate years at the University of Alberta attending Tory rallies with Joe Clark. (He also spent three years in the South Pacific as a Mormon missionary.) He was teaching law at UBC when Judge Nathan Nemetz brought him to Premier Dave Barrett's attention. Matkin was first hired by Barrett to sit on a three-man committee to advise government on the disputatious labour movement; eventually he became deputy minister of labour. (Jim Kinnaird became his associate deputy after resigning his job as head of the Building Trades Council.) Matkin easily survived the transition to a Social Credit government and became deputy minister at Intergovernmental Relations, the ministry that Bennett used as his think-tank, first for his constitutional forays and then in developing his restraint program. Jim Matkin was the brains behind the public-sector wage-restraint program, the Rubber Room Dave Barrett had promised to unload if he won the election.

Matkin will tell you that for his first few months at the Employers' Council he was uncertain, feeling his way. As a result, he proved to be an apologist for government.

That alignment of circumstances in the summer of 1983 allowed Bill Bennett to capitalize further on his election win.

Michael Walker's joy was obvious as he wrote about the budget in a newspaper column a few days later. On the abolition of rent controls: "there are few instances in the western industrialized world of governments who have had the foresight and political courage to abandon this form of intervention." The legislation to terminate government workers "without cause" was music to his ears: "It provides a clear indication of the government's firm determination, and may act in British Columbia as a Canada-wide precedent of the kind of singlemindedness which Ronald Reagan displayed in dealing with the air traffic controllers."

He was also pleased with the government's big-bang strategy. Dropping the legislation and the budget all at once without consultation caught the opposition completely off guard. It was just what he recommended at Okanagan Lake, he says. He didn't advise them to raise taxes or what to do on social legislation, but he told them to do whatever they were going to do in "one swell foop .... There is nothing known about how to implement a policy of restraint; there is something known about how special-interest groups respond." And then he referred them to Mancur Olson.

What Walker didn't know was that there had been a strategy to consult with the groups that would be affected by the legislation. Plans were laid out for meetings between ministers and union leaders, tenant groups, and consumer associations. But a couple of key ministers, provincial secretary Jim Chabot, and the minister responsible for consumer services and the Rentalsman's office, Jim Hewitt, balked and begged off. They told Bennett they had nothing to consult about. A government that won three successive elections without talking to the community shouldn't start now. Those advisers pushing this strategy argued that all Chabot and Hewitt had to do was showbiz – walk in the room, shake hands, smile, and say things are really tough – all under the watchful eye of the TV cameras. No dice.

The big-bang strategy even caught Milton Friedman's eye. He was particularly impressed that Bennett ran a whole election campaign without letting on what he had in mind. He immortalized Bennett's stroke of brilliance in *The Tyranny of the Status Quo*, which deals with four governments: Reagan's America, Thatcher's Britain, Mitterrand's France, and Bill Bennett's British Columbia.

Immediately after his reelection [Bennett] announced a sweeping program to ... cut the number of government employees by 25 percent and to reduce spending on a wide range of programs. In addition, he abolished outright a number of politically sensitive commissions. ...

Now, Mr. Bennett could have introduced these measures before the election .... Why didn't he? The answer is so obvious that it is embarrassing to spell it out, yet it is crucial to understanding the ... tyranny of the status quo. Any measure that affects a *concentrated* group significantly ... tends to have effects on individual members of that group that are substantial, occur promptly, and are highly visible. The effects of the same measure on ... a *diffused* group ... tend to be trivial, longer delayed, and less visible. Quick, concentrated reaction is the major source of strength of special interest groups .... It motivates politicians to make grandiose promises to such special interests before an election – and to postpone any measures adversely affecting special interest groups until after an election.

Had Premier Bennett spelled out his intention ... before the election, he would have aroused immediate and vocal opposition from the special interest groups affected – and only lukewarm and far less vocal enthusiasm from taxpayers in general. By waiting until after the election ... Premier Bennett could hope that the bad effects on the concentrated groups would dissipate before the next election while the good effects on the broad constituency would have time both to take effect and to be recognized as the result of the measures he took.

Friedman concludes his praise of Bill Bennett's strategy by claiming that Bennett had no choice. "It may well be that a majority of the electorate – if well informed – would approve the measures before, as well as after, the election. But the minorities specially affected have strong incentives to mount a propaganda barrage to assure that the majority are not well informed. . . .''

While hardly a vote of confidence in democracy and open government, Milton Friedman, Mancur Olson and Michael Walker all agreed on the effect of Bennett's strategy: protest by the gored special-interest groups. But they didn't figure on that unique alignment of events in the summer of 1983 – the vacuum of power on the left and the zeal with which Bill Bennett pursued his goal. This alignment created an equally unique reaction. Solidarity.

Within hours of the Tough Guy's revolutionary assault, the province began to polarize as never before. The polarization that was so integral to Bill Bennett's political style and B.C.'s social fabric led to the biggest extra-parliamentary opposition in Canadian history. Within hours people were on the phones. Within days organizational meetings were held. Within weeks people who had never been involved in politics found a common cause and took to the streets.

9

SOLIDARITY FOREVER

Reaction to Bill Bennett's revolution was immediate and widespread. In the East, Peter C. Newman, busy writing his *Debrett's Illustrated Guide to the Canadian Establishment*, digressed from detailing the foibles of the rich and powerful to give his assessment of the B.C. scene:

> In the late spring of 1983 the jerry-rigged hierarchy that runs the place received an unexpected boost with the electoral coronation of Bill Bennett, who interpreted the voters' rejection of Dave Barrett-style socialism as a mandate to bring back the 13th century.

If Bennett expected support from the investment community he would certainly not find comfort in a report in the *Wall Street Journal*. The strategy of winning an election by stealth that Milton Friedman found so charming smelled like trouble to the people who write for the tycoons of America:

> Mr. Bennett's opponents claim, with justification, that the electorate didn't know what it was voting for. Of course, if he did define his austerity measures in advance he would have risked losing the election. But at least the electoral process would have resolved the matter. Now, Premier Bennett's opponents haven't any weapons except labor turmoil.

In British Columbia, the social-services cuts, the firings, and the legislation attacking unions and diminishing human rights unleashed a flood of opposition energy. Before the July 8 weekend had passed, the B.C. branch of the Consumers' Association of Canada made a suggestion. As the government had cut funding for consumer groups and most consumer services were wiped out, the Ministry of Consumer and Corporate Affairs should be renamed simply the Ministry of Corporate Affairs. There was no way, they argued, that the private sector was willing or able to take over responsibility for the services that had been chopped. Traditionally bickering women's groups quickly united under the banner Women Against the Budget. The Government Employees' Union hardly seemed hyberbolic in suggesting that Bennett's barrage was "one of the worst attacks on human rights and freedoms ever mounted by a democratically elected government in the western world." The British Columbia Nurses' Union called Bennett's laws "immoral", adding that "once again the provincial government has acted destructively and without prior consultation in the name of holy restraint. It has wiped out individual rights having nothing to do with saving taxpayers' money; it has made permanent second-class citizens of public employees, and it has ignored the erosion of B.C. health care." Various comparisons were drawn with the Solidarity trade unionists in Poland, much to the dismay of people of liberal sensibility, who couldn't imagine Bill Bennett as the General Wojciech Jaruzelski of British Columbia.

Bennett responded glibly that these groups were simply refighting the May 5 election.

There was a mad scramble to harness the growing protest. On July 4, George Hewison, secretary of the communist-influenced Fishermen's Union and chairman of the Vancouver and District Labour Council's Unemployed Action Committee, called a meeting for July 11 in anticipation of a nasty Socred budget. When Hewison phoned B.C. Federation of Labour president Art Kube the day after the budget, Kube told him he had nothing definite planned for the BCFed. Hewison expected that fifteen to twenty community and labour representatives would turn up at his meeting, so he booked the boardroom at the Fishermen's Hall.

More than ninety people representing teachers, trade unions, women's groups, the church, seniors, and tenants jammed into the room. By the time the meeting was over they had formed the Lower Mainland Budget Coalition. They fired off a telegram to the NDP Opposition in Victoria telling them to block the legislation in any way they could. They called on the BCFed to organize a province-wide coalition and to mount a protest. Then they cranked up the machinery for their own protest rally in the lower mainland. They figured they could draw five thousand people to the B.C. Place parking lot on July 23.

That same day, July 11, Kube met with the officers of the BCFed and presented an action program that he had knocked out in twenty minutes. Within the week there would be an unprecedented meeting of all federation affiliates and non-affiliates, including the B.C. Teachers' Federation, hospital workers, and independent Canadian unions. Kube said talk of a general strike was "somewhat premature".

Talk of the communists scooping the social democrats running the BCFed was everywhere, however. The old rivalries between these two forces practically overshadowed the need for an effective strategy. The boys at the BCFed weren't sure where all this activity was going, but they wanted to run the operation; and they certainly didn't want to follow a communist agenda. On July 14 Kube made an urgent phone call to George Hewison. He wanted Hewison to call off the Lower Mainland Budget Coalition demonstration. Kube said he was worried that it would be a flop. After all, it had taken the labour movement four months of organizing back in 1976 to get 12,000 people out to protest the federal government's wage and price controls. And here Hewison's coalition was trying to pull off a demonstration in less than two weeks. Hewison said Kube would have to convince the coalition's steering committee the next morning at Fishermen's Hall. The next morning at Fishermen's Hall Kube was creamed.

That afternoon Kube chaired a defiant meeting at the Operating Engineers Hall, and Operation Solidarity was born. (The social democrats in the crowd had their chuckle when the meeting approved the name Solidarity, an obvious barb thrown at the communists and their buddies running the Polish government.) Art Kube was the driving force in the decision to organize and fund a coalition of community groups and rallies under the Solidarity banner. He knew instinctively that this would give any protest by trade unions added punch.

Right after that first Operation Solidarity meeting he got in touch with Renate Shearer, one of the human rights commissioners unloaded to make way for Bennett's New Social Order. She was also a community organizer and social planner, who had worked for the City of Vancouver and the YWCA. When the budget hit, Shearer organized human-rights activists all over the province to explain what had happened to the commission and the Human Rights Branch. Kube asked her to meet with Clay Perry of the IWA, Jean Swanson from the Hospital Employees' Union, Gene Errington of (CUPE), the Canadian Union of Public Employees and Bill Black, a law professor at UBC with a particular interest in human-rights legislation. Together they would form the core group of the Solidarity Coalition. The coalition was headed by a triumvirate: Shearer, Kube, and Father Jim Roberts, a radical Catholic theologian. The labour unions in Operation Solidarity gave the new coalition a budget of $20,000 a month, free printing, and a fistful of organizers. The coalition set up an office, picked up a few scraps of furniture, and went to work.

As Kube and Hewison attempted to harness the growing protest, the Socreds were planning a second wave of firings. On the day that Hewison and the Lower Mainland Budget Coalition were crammed into the boardroom at Fishermen's Hall, regional managers from the ministry of human resources were being told that within twenty-four hours 350 permanent staff and more than 200 auxiliaries would get the axe. Services eliminated would include a post-partum counselling service, the teams set up to help social workers and families deal with child abuse, programs to help the mentally retarded, daycare services, support staff in regional ministry offices, and family support workers, who keep children and their parents together. This would bring the total firings since budget day to 1,000.

Early that afternoon, as Kube was ending his press conference announcing the birth of Solidarity and Hewison was winding down his meeting, the Human Resources deputy minister was summoned from his meeting of regional managers and told that the firings would be put on hold for a week.

A week later, on July 18, there was another order to wait, the first of many stalls in firings throughout the civil service that would cause government work to seize up for months.

That same day Provincial Secretary Jim Chabot, the minister responsible for the public service, had a short, high-pitched screaming match with public-sector union leaders. He said he would consider introducing regulations for his "terminate without cause" legislation that would make some allowances for seniority. The union leaders wanted the legislation dropped. During the altercation, government offices in Prince George, Terrace, Kamloops, and Victoria were shut down by fired government workers who threw up picket lines for the day. More than three hundred workers stayed off the job.

The following day in Kamloops, government workers at the Tranquille institution for the severely physically and mentally handicapped occupied four buildings. (The occupation was to last for twenty-one days.) Denials by the minister of finance on budget day that Tranquille would be shut down now appeared to have been less than accurate. The workers were protesting government plans to move the 325 residents into smaller private community facilities well ahead of the original 1991 date for closing. While most people, including the B.C. Association for the Mentally Retarded, agreed with this program of deinstitutionalization, they questioned the speed with which it would be done. The government was also breaking its contract with the BCGEU by dumping the workers. The government would not save a nickel by "privatizing" these services, but more than 600 government jobs would be chopped in the ministry's attempts to meet Bennett's target of a 25 per cent reduction in the public service within eighteen months.

That week, Bill Hamilton stepped down as president of the Employers' Council of British Columbia. After ten years as the leading spokesman for big business in the province, this former postmaster general in the Diefenbaker cabinet was moving on to the Macdonald Commission on the economy. The day of his going-away banquet was, as Hamilton recalls, "one of the most difficult situations of my lifetime". At the afternoon meeting of the Employers' Council board of directors he explained that he was appalled by the implications of the Socred budget, particularly by what was happening to human rights. The government's goal of reducing government spending was admirable, but "their proposed techniques of reaching them are not going to achieve that goal. They are nothing but divisive and destructive."

Hamilton said he really couldn't leave his job without making his views known, and he planned to do so at that evening's testimonial dinner at the Bayshore. His board was not amused. He recalls that they were "shocked because the head table included Bill Bennett and Jack Munro", the head of the IWA. The meeting was long, tense, and emotional. When the board failed to convince Hamilton to button his lip, a couple of his close friends on the board pursued him into his office and continued the debate. While they agreed with much of what he had to say, they argued that he would only embarrass and bring down Bennett's wrath on the business community by speaking up.

Hamilton remained unconvinced. For as long as Bill Bennett had been premier there had been tension between them. Bennett did not take criticism well. He had never confronted Hamilton directly but instead had complained to Hamilton's board members. More than once Hamilton had been aware of Bill Bennett putting on the pressure to squeeze him out of the job. Dealing with Bennett was not like dealing with the federal government. When you deal with Bennett, "everything is measured in partisan terms." In Bill Bennett's British Columbia "the business community does not have an independent voice." That night, after the meal and the sherbet, and the announcement that $100,000 was being contributed in Bill Hamilton's name to endow a chair in labour relations at the University of British Columbia, Bill Hamilton told Bill Bennett and 150 other people that he thought Bennett's restraint crusade was ill-conceived. The story was in the next morning's *Province*.

On July 18, more than four hundred people packed the auditorium at Fishermen's Hall for the first general meeting of the Lower Mainland Budget Coalition. The debate started with a motion by Gerry Scott, a former NDP candidate and Dave Barrett executive assistant. Scott moved that the NDP be invited to appear on the platform of the coalition rally planned for the next Saturday. (Scott was at the meeting with NDP MP Ian Waddell and NDP MLA Bob Skelly.) The NDP were as nervous as organized labour that this protest was getting away from them. Their natural constituency was in no hurry to turn to either the NDP or the B.C. Federation of Labour for leadership. Most of the crowd, including many NDPers and trade unionists, had had it up to the armpits with electoral politics, and the labour movement had never been a great friend of community groups. The motion was defeated; the NDP was told to stick to the legislature and block those bills.

On the afternoon of Saturday, July 23, the sun was shining, the breeze was blowing, and the birds were singing in the trees as a boisterous crowd gathered at the CN station just east of Main Street and marched over the Georgia Street viaduct to B.C. Place. The rally that hoped to draw five thousand people and that Kube worried would flop attracted more than twenty thousand people by police estimates and closer to thirty-five thousand according to rally organizers. It was the beginning of the hottest political summer in the province's history.

On July 22 the four-day-old government workers' occupation at Tranquille had expanded to all ten administrative buildings and the farmland operated by the institution about a mile away; the patients received services as usual. But the government refused to discuss their plans to wind down the operation until the occupation ended. A stalemate.

The on-again, off-again firing of the ministry of human resources workers was on again. On July 25, the deputy minister sent out letters to the "redundant" workers telling them they were finished as of November 1, the end of the union contract. Until then they were to keep doing their jobs. The government would get back to them "as soon as possible".

On Wednesday morning, July 27, Art Kube had breakfast with Bennett's deputy minister, Norman Spector. This was the first of Spector's diplomatic forays to separate the labour movement from the community groups in Solidarity by shifting the trade-union focus away from the legislation dealing with tenant and human rights and on to strictly labour issues. This time Spector failed.

That afternoon, a small contingent of RCMP officers inside the legislature locked all the entrances, and a security guard was placed at the main entrance. At 3:00 P.M. protestors started to arrive, first in small groups and then in droves. They covered the lawns, surrounded the flower beds, and spilled over into the streets. There were banners condemning the budget cuts and posters calling Bennett a fascist. There were people standing and singing "We Shall Overcome", and people in wheelchairs shouting against the government. This first Operation Solidarity rally exceeded the organizers' expectations.

As the speakers lined up at the microphone on the legislature steps Dave Barrett appeared in the doorway and worked his way along the steps toward the podium. He looked nervous, out of place. He was not an invited guest. Solidarity carried on the Lower Mainland Budget Coalition's policy of excluding official NDP participation from its meetings and rallies. Art Kube gave in to scattered shouts from the crowd and asked Barrett to say a few words. But when Barrett spoke there was no passion, nothing to match the anger of the demonstrators. He spoke of peaceful parliamentary solutions. He told them that they had come in peace and that they should go in peace. His pacifist advice was quickly elbowed aside for something livelier.

The NDP caucus was in a decided funk. Their frustration grew as Solidarity captured headlines and was increasingly perceived to be the real opposition to Bennett's restraint revolution. During the three weeks after the budget was brought down the NDP managed to block what few bills the government introduced. If the government had any strategy it was to say nothing: no government member rose to speak in favour of the legislation.

The government seemed very tentative. They introduced Bill 3, the legislation that allowed them to fire civil servants without cause; then they withdrew it and introduced the innocuous Tobacco Tax Amendment Act; then they introduced Bill 3 again. The great urgency of July 7 was gone. It was as if they had no plan despite their belief a month earlier that the whole package would be passed by August 1.

A decision to send ministers around the province to defend and explain the legislation was scrapped. The Socreds figured that the demonstrations would play themselves out and the NDP would roll over and allow the legislation to pass. Bill Hamilton notwithstanding, the Socreds were still finding lots of folks who were telling them that they were on the right track. As long as the target was an overweight public service and uncontrolled union greed, the Socreds had all the support they needed.

In Ottawa that summer Bill Bennett and British Columbia were a regular item on the Liberal cabinet agenda. Trudeau's principal secretary, Tom Axworthy, had assigned two people from the Prime Minister's Office to move out to the coast and stay in touch with the Solidarity movement. Cabinet discussions centred on two areas. The first was the need for Ottawa to step in and fund groups being cut completely by Bennett's restraint program. The second was the political advantage of openly criticizing Bennett. While the Liberals had lauded his wage-restraint program back in February 1982, this stuff was offensive. Characterizing Bill Bennett's neo-conservative revolution as the leading edge of what any future Tory government would do to Canada was mouthwatering, but no concerted plan of attack was worked out.

However, individual federal ministers began to respond. Finance Minister Marc Lalonde called Bennett's budget "radical" and "extreme". Judy Erola, the minister responsible for women, fired off a hot little missive denouncing social-services cuts and the massacre in the Human Rights Branch. Senator Ray Perrault, the minister of fitness and amateur sport, looked at the plan to unload 25 per cent of the public service and said, "I don't understand how it can be implemented without substantial legal action on the part of certain members of the civil service."

Federal Labour Minister Charles Caccia predicted that the proposed legislation would trigger complaints to the International Labor Organization, the United Nations-related body that monitors workers' rights and freedoms. Caccia sent a telegram to B.C. Labour Minister Bob McClelland asking the government "to rethink its position on these bills and sustain its reputation of recognizing the need to protect fundamental freedoms and rights of all citizens of the province."

The Socreds considered the source of the criticism and went on the attack. When Ottawa funded a small group of human-rights activists on Vancouver Island, the Socreds accused the feds of undermining a democratically elected government.

In early August amendments were introduced to Bill 3, The Public Sector Restraint Act. The "fire without cause" clause was removed, and a clause allowing negotiated layoff criteria was written in amidst nervous denials of responsibility for the provocative phrase that had helped spark the upheaval in the streets. Norman Spector was the most frequent target for the blame within the senior public service, although Bennett's instinct had obviously failed him as well. Spector was the policy brains-trust on that particular piece of work, although he tried to fob off the legislative drafting blunder on "poor legal advice the government took".

Under the amendments a number of circumstances, including organizational changes and the elimination of programs, would allow an employee to be unloaded. The Socreds pointed at the amendments as an example of how the consultative process worked. But the effect wasn't much different, and the damage had already been done.

For the people in Solidarity and the Lower Mainland Budget Coalition, August was a blur of meetings, "fifty a fucking day", according to Jack Munro. But what sustained the energy of the movement were the rallies. The most dramatic event of the summer took place on the afternoon of August 10 at Empire Stadium. Close to 40,000 people were on their feet in the stands when government workers left their jobs and transit workers shut down the bus system and marched into the stadium. And when the uniformed firemen's band came in and marched around the track people actually had tears in their eyes.

Dave Barrett's mother, Rose, was there, caught up in the emotion of the event. She told her son afterwards that this was the beginning of the revolution that she had worked so many years for. IWA executive and NDP party president Gerry Stoney perched up in the stands to watch it all go by. "It was the spontaneity of ordinary people being there," he recalled. "Not IWA jackets, not BCGEU jackets, and not transit workers – but just ordinary people standing there saying: 'We're mad.' "

The demonstration went on too long, though. After two hours, the transit workers had to leave and start up their buses for the rush hour. By the time the last speaker droned to the end of the last speech the stadium was half empty. The problem was organization, and it would plague Solidarity for months to come. The community groups and the more militant types in the Lower Mainland Budget Coalition wanted music and celebration. The trade-union leadership wanted their traditional speeches and messages of fraternal greetings. The awkward compromise produced an ungainly event.

That split over organizing tactics erupted in an unpleasant Operation Solidarity meeting at the BCFed offices twelve days later. Women Against the Budget were planning a demonstration in front of Human Resources Minister Grace McCarthy's home in the tree-lined opulence of Shaughnessy Heights. Such guerilla theatre was standard action for community groups but totally foreign to the more staid trade-union movement. Frances Wasserlein was at the meeting defending the Women Against the Budget position.

> Many of the trade unionists objected strongly to organizing a demonstration in front of someone's house on all kinds of largely specious grounds. People stood up and said how terrible it was for them when they were a little kid and their father was the manager of a factory and there was a strike and the strikers came and picketed in front of their house. And these were trade unionists, right, saying these things! People stood up and said that it was unconscionable and an attack and blah, blah, blah, and they would be unwilling to support such a demonstration.

Five days later the demonstration went ahead. The Stone Soup Luncheon they called it, to echo the Dirty Thirties when people with little more than a few vegetables would get together and make a communal soup meal. A women's band sang from a portable stage while soup was served, and people danced in the street. In the middle of the celebration an old man in a white Mercedes sedan ignored the police road block on Beverley Crescent and drove through the demonstrating tenants, lesbians, welfare mothers, kids, and seniors, leaning on his horn. He rolled down the window just long enough to denounce them all as "Communists".

Bishop Remi De Roo joined the attack against Bennett and his radical legislation. The liberal Roman Catholic bishop said Bennett's restraint program was evil: "I'm sure the government never set out to create an evil program. But they don't realize their narrow conservative approach . . . is creating suffering," he said. "There is disorder built into the structure of the government's program that is evil, and the evil lies in the fact of people being hurt." The Tough Guy came back in true partisan form. The bishop, he growled, "doesn't trust the private sector, he doesn't believe in profits. He believes the answer is to be found in larger governments."

Frank Miller, then treasurer of Ontario and on the road to replace Bill Davis briefly as premier, made an observation that was announced by a trade unionist from the podium of a Solidarity rally: "I'm watching what's happening with extreme trepidation. If Bennett succeeds, I think every government will end up doing the same in its own way. If he fails, the cause of government restraint will have been set back for a decade. Either way there's an awful lot riding on what's happening out there."

Jim Matkin, the new president of the Employers' Council, called for an end to the confrontation sweeping the province. On the eve of demonstrations planned for Nanaimo and Kelowna, Matkin said: "We are not happy with what is going on. It has an unsettling effect on everyone."

Three weeks later, on September 16, amid growing concern that Solidarity was fizzling, more than eighty people occupied the government's cabinet offices in Vancouver. The plan was organized by half a dozen unions and four community groups. Members of the BCGEU provided floor plans of the government offices. The Operation Solidarity leadership had known an occupation was being planned – they thought a welfare office was going to be hit – but had not officially sanctioned it: another split between the moderates and the radicals in Solidarity. Most of the people in the occupation didn't know what their target was until moments before they reached the doors in Robson Square;

they were told only to assemble on a downtown street corner that morning and bring along their sleeping bags. Socreds automatically accused the NDP of supporting this illegal act; the NDP said nothing.

The atmosphere in the occupied cabinet offices was made-for-TV festive. Jack Gerow, chief spokesman for the Hospital Employees' Union, delivered late-night pizza. Bill Bennett refused to be baited into forcibly ending the occupation. He simply deplored it, and most British Columbians agreed with him. Twenty-seven hours later it was over. A small demonstration greeted the occupation force emerging into Robson Square.

By September the legislature in Victoria had become an armed camp. The RCMP had a command post in a small room in the basement and would often be sitting in the public galleries watching the debate and keeping an eye on observers drawn to the heat developing on the floor of the chamber. Bill Bennett was regularly escorted by two RCMP bodyguards; Socred MLAs always locked their doors when they left their offices.

The legislative clerical staff was run through the RCMP's special lecture series on terrorist attacks. They were shown a slide presentation depicting the remains of bombed buildings, bodies dismembered by explosions, letter bombs, telephone bombs, and bombs activated by opening doors. The briefing was requested following threats on the lives of government members. On September 21 a bomb scare drew the Department of National Defence bomb squad to the mail room. There they discovered a box of unarmed B.C. Rail coffee cups destined for the minister of finance.

On September 19 the Tough Guy makes his move. After drifting aimlessly through the summer, he gives the order that the house will be run around the clock. All night sittings, legislation by exhaustion: his father's old strategy. Democracy can be such a bother. He must get his major bills passed by October 31, when the BCGEU contract expires. He intimates privately that the latest opinion polls show him growing in popularity. Solidarity and its NDP soulmates are on the skids.

Bill 3, The Public Sector Restraint Act, the renovated "fire without cause" bill, is brought back for debate for the first time since August 16. Dave Barrett rises as the party's designated speaker. (This means he can speak until his voice or bladder fails him.) When debate on this bill was adjourned more than a month earlier, he had warmed the air for three hours and twenty-six minutes.

House Speaker Walter Davidson waves Barrett back to his seat. When Barrett looks puzzled, Walter slips him a note: "Trust me." Before Barrett can begin to speak a So-cred is on his feet with a point of order, the lead of a one-two punch. The right cross comes from Davidson. The rules of the house appear to change. You can be a designated speaker some of the time, but you can't be a designated speaker all of the time. Barrett is blocked from carrying on the debate. He jumps up and down in protest. Davidson orders him out of the house. Barrett leaves.

The Opposition settle in. They divide their ranks into three teams and turn up one morning sporting A, B, and C buttons. Each team works a four-hour shift in the house. (The Socreds' buttons simply read, "The Winning Team".) During the first week NDP MLA Gordon Hanson puts in a nine-hour shift; the debate runs through the night and into the morning. While some look on and others sleep at their desks, he hammers away at the government on Bill 3. As time passes, Hanson's voice draws thin as a string, his eyes blur from reading anything available to fill the time with noise. His desk is littered with oral aids: lozenges, glasses of juice, throat spray. Finally he succumbs.

A small pack of neophyte Socred backbenchers re-lentlessly heckle any NDPer who dares to speak. These are the Yahoos, swearing, spitting, and snarling: at the waste of time, the cost of keeping the house sitting, the quality of the socialist argument. Cabinet ministers provide photo opportunities slumbering in their offices on couches or army cots. Forestry Minister Tom Waterland brings his teddy bear when he turns up to vote. The Opposition tries to twist rules of order, points of procedure, points of personal privilege, demands for adjournment, challenges to the chair – anything to extend the debate, stall the legislation, or force a vote, which would drag ministers back to the legislative chamber from their slumber, their card games, or their office work.

This cradle of democratic interplay is effectively reduced by Bill Bennett's war against the Opposition to a madhouse, with bomb squads on the alert, public access severely limited, increased body searches, and police watching sleep-starved inmates howling at the moon.

As BCTV cameraman Russ Clifford recalls, by the night of October 5, "everyone was really wacko". Some time before midnight, the Socred whip, Elwood Vietch, becomes annoyed by a BCTV news report. He comes running up the stairs to the press gallery screaming outrageously for "that lying son of a whore" BCTV legislative reporter Clem Chapple. The mood has even infected the normally unflappable *Hansard* clerks. In an unprecedented act of editorial comment the *Hansard* blues, the rough draft of the debate, appears with a fist-sized angry dragon on the heretofore pristine front cover. Disgust. Within twenty-four hours, British Columbia will make parliamentary history.

The tension between the media and the Socreds has not been limited to the Socred whip and the BCTV reporter. A week earlier Speaker Walter Davidson blocked TV cameras and tape-recorders from the corridor in front of the main entrances to the legislative chamber. (The B.C. legislature is the only seat of government west of the Maritimes that does not allow regular broadcasts of any debate.) It was in this corridor that reporters traditionally interviewed politicians before or after their appearance in the House. The clearing of the corridor was inspired by an amusing TV documentary of snoozing, snoring Socred MLAS, filmed through the leaded glass doors of the legislature by Russ Clifford. Not the sort of thing the folks at home should see.

Yahoos in the Socred back benches continue to harangue the eternally disputatious Opposition, but the Socreds, led by ex-Liberal shipjumper and minister of science fiction Pat

McGeer, decide that closure is the answer. This usually rare parliamentary practice is being used like cheap wine on Skid Row.

At 3:40 A.M. on October 6, 1983, reporters are awakened by the ruckus on the floor of the legislature. A leading Socred Yahoo, John Parks, has just taken the speaker's chair, and Barrett is on his feet trying to challenge a ruling on a motion to adjourn. The NDP wants an adjournment; Parks isn't interested. The NDP is challenging the chair partly to force a recorded vote: the bells would sound throughout the legislative precincts and force sleeping cabinet ministers to rouse themselves, gather up their teddy bears, and plod down to the chamber. But Barrett is discovering that Parks is no longer making rulings, he is "interpreting the application" of a rule. No "ruling", no challenge. No challenge, no bells. As he was two weeks earlier, Barrett is being blocked.

Barrett goes for broke, joined by the meanest, shrewdest bit of business in the Opposition, NDP MLA Frank Howard. Parks is in over his head. First Barrett, then Howard, carries on in a bullying, belligerent fashion, seeking – with some success – to confuse and confound Parks. At least four times Parks asks for procedural advice from the Clerk of the House. At 4:20 A.M. Parks orders Barrett to leave the chamber. Quietly. Frank Howard is speaking when Barrett turns and whispers loudly to him: "They'll have to carry me out chair and all. That's bullshit. I told him to give me some room to manoeuvre." Barrett suggests that Parks call a recess. In one of the interminable delays, Barrett tells his colleagues that if this keeps up he knows he's going to get the toss. They say that if it feels good go for it.

By 4:30 A.M. Walter Davidson is flapping about in his black robes in the Forbidden Corridor. He is listening in on the debate, talking with the sergeants-at-arms, and warning off the small collection of reporters and cameramen gathered for the impending event.

Inside the chamber Parks and Barrett are nose to nose. Parks finally orders the sergeants-at-arms, Jack Dunn and Bill Roach, to move on Barrett. Barrett drops into his chair as the blue-coated men come toward him. Twice Parks orders them to escort Barrett from the chamber. Barrett refuses to move. Parks checks with the Clerk of the House for advice.

One of the Yahoos yells, "Get the cameras. He wants the rest of the day off." Another starts up with, "Anarchy here we go." NDP MLA Bob Skelly moves up to the empty chair beside Barrett to block his passage if they try to drag him out of the house.

Parks orders the sergeants-at-arms to remove Barrett, once and then again. The sergeants each grab Barrett by an arm, but he keeps his grip on the chair. Skelly moves out of the way at Barrett's request before Barrett, chair and all, is dragged toward the door backwards. The Yahoos are screaming, "Get the cameras . . . a leader that's going down the tube may as well go backwards." The Opposition is on its feet, slightly stunned.

In the hallway Davidson is threatening the press, waving them away as they ask if they can record the first time in British parliamentary history that a former premier and leader of the Opposition is hauled bodily from the chamber.

At 4:35 A.M., the chair falls away from Barrett as he is dragged through the revolving doors. Davidson is screaming and waving his arms frantically at a print reporter who is holding his microphone toward Barrett: "I won't allow you to put that on air." Barrett hits the floor and looks shocked. No TV lights, no cameras. Then he is on his feet, hollering at Davidson, trembling with fury. This is "an absurd, obscene abuse of freedoms of a parliamentary democracy." He will be banished until the end of the session.

On Wednesday, October 12, Bill 3 was passed, after ten closure motions, fifty-four recorded votes, and twenty-one hours of debate.

The house was adjourned so the Socreds could flee to Vancouver and celebrate at their annual convention. During his keynote address to more than a thousand enthusiastic supporters, Bennett was unbending:

Today, I want to tell those who oppose us, special-interest groups, that while they may have concerns, we will listen, as we have. We will listen to every British Columbian and listen to their advice. We will accept their op – [he stumbles]. . . . We will give them the opportunity to consult. We will give them every opportunity to help us provide better government. But we will never back down on the policies that we advocate. We look for strength. We look for improvement, but we will not back down on what we set out to do.

When the MLAs were introduced to the convention delegates, John Parks was given an ovation second only to Bennett's. At the annual fund-raising auction, his boot, presumably the one he put to Barrett, was auctioned off for $1,195. It was purchased by Pam Clarke-Saari, from Mission in the Fraser Valley Bible Belt, as a gift for her father. She said she wanted to be part of B.C. history.

The next day, Saturday, October 15, Solidarity mounted its biggest protest ever. Again there was a split on tactics. The moderate trade unions wanted to call it off. They were worried that they wouldn't be able to exceed the numbers at previous rallies. They were also worried that they could end up with a riot. (Two years earlier angry demonstrators stormed a Socred convention, and things got pretty messy.) But they had no better plan, and they weren't getting anywhere with Bennett. So the march was planned for 10:30 A.M.

People from ninety-seven trade unions and community groups started forming up at designated locations in a seven-square-block area near the B.C. Place stadium. There were enough police to control a European soccer crowd. At 10:30, more than 50,000 marched past the Socred convention at the Hotel Vancouver, shouting and shaking their fists in a vain attempt to exorcise their devil. This throng was the real opposition in B.C., disenfranchised, driven into the streets. A few Socred delegates came out and exchanged words with the demonstrators. "You

Commie." "You Fascist." But most stayed a few floors above and mocked the crowd, the losers.

The Vancouver *Province* gave the demonstration only a few lines of print. The *Sun* ran a photo that made it look as if the protest was being led by a small delegation that was actually at some distance from the front of the procession: the Communist Party of Canada.

10
A VERBAL
AGREEMENT

On Wednesday, October 12, 1983, the day that Bill 3 was
finally forced through the legislature, the Tough Guy sat in
his office with his closest staff members to lay out his
strategy for the next phase. He was cool and he was precise.
His most important piece of legislation, which gave him
the power to fire public servants without serious impedi-
ment from their union, was now past the debate stage. It
would be proclaimed before he got into negotiations with
the Government Employees' Union. He had no further use
for the charade of parliament.

Bill 2, the bill that would gut the BCGEU's collective
agreement, would be kept around as a handy club. There
would be no further debate on it, as Bennett had no intention of pushing it through. He was a general fighting on two
fronts: in the House and in the streets. In nine days he
would shut down one front, the legislature. A "cooling-off
period", he announced in province-wide free television
time. Once again he ignored the legislature; even his cabinet ministers weren't told until the day before the
announcement.

What his pollsters had been telling him confirmed a Vancouver *Sun* poll conducted in the middle of September:

while most people in B.C. didn't like the way Bennett was implementing his restraint program, most saw the need for government restraint in spending. More important, the poll results said Solidarity was not winning the battle for the hearts and minds of British Columbians. As pollster Marty Goldfarb said, "the concept of Solidarity serves his [Bennett's] purposes . . . . It smacks of a totalitarian regime. The people are not prepared to accept that [that's what Bennett's government is] . . . . It just leads to his strength. As long as they keep that name they're helping him." Polarization fed by the fear of anarchy.

During the next few days Bennett's rhetoric took on a harder edge. The man who once quipped that he would "never say never" now insisted that he would "never back down" from his chosen course. Amid a loving, laughing audience at the Socred convention he rose to new heights of messianic fervour. He and his willing wordsmith, Norman Spector, had dusted off all the old John Kennedy clichés. Bennett now rarely mangled his metaphors. He no longer "spoke [his] mind straight from the shoulder." A favourite new line was a shameless twist on a thought by Lord Acton. "The one pervading evil of democracy," the British peer allowed, "is the tyranny of the majority or rather that party, not always the majority, that succeeds by force or fraud in carrying elections." This sentiment, in Bennett's mouth, became the "tyranny of the minority" and was amusingly sewn together with former Black Panther Eldridge Cleaver's contention that, "if you're not part of the solution you're part of the problem."

Bill Bennett hurled these missiles with some skill at his opposition – Solidarity – nurturing the impression of a democratically elected government under siege by the rabble in the streets. The thick batch of Socred party propaganda, *Recovery '83*, cranked out to give the "facts" and to counter charges against government policy, ignored the NDP. Solidarity was the force to be reckoned with. When the NDP came into Bennett's critical view, it was merely out of habit. Their leader sat in Victoria in a self-righteous funk, mulling over his future, and his party was terrified that Bennett would call an election. NDP president Gerry Stoney knew that if Bennett went to the people over a general strike led by Solidarity, the socialists would be obliterated.

Hours before Bennett took to the airwaves to adjourn the legislature "indefinitely", workers in the Rentalsman's offices around the province got their second reprieve in a month; the firings planned for September 30 and delayed until October 31 were now postponed until the end of November. The day the House closed, the NDP, in one last flail of resistance, released a leaked internal ministry of labour report that said the Socred restraint program was dampening consumer demand and hurting the economy. (Private-sector economists, including those with the Conference Board of Canada, soon came to the same conclusion.)

Bennett's TV performance was a brilliant combination of hard-luck story and attack, the only time an election campaign has been fought by a government after the people have gone to the polls. He attacked the federal government for not spending more money on social programs in British Columbia. A few breaths later, he attacked them for spending too much money and "not living within the taxpayers' means." Contradiction just enlivened the speech.

He also attacked the public service, the same public service he had expanded while the rest of the economy shrank: "Public-sector workers cannot be in a privileged position and must be prepared to bear their fair share of the recession." Rather than dwell on his government's role in this conundrum, he played the public-sector unions against their private-sector comrades.

> Lifetime job security does not exist in the private sector, as the 100,000 jobs lost during the recession demonstrate. More than one of every three forest workers . . . more than one of every four resource workers and more than one of every five manufacturing, service, and professional workers who were laid off during the recession are still not back at work today. During the

same period, the number of people working in the public sector actually increased.

This was not lost on Jack Munro and his IWA members.

Winners write history, in British Columbia as elsewhere. In his address Bennett reiterated the myth that critics of his legislation refuse to consult. Most jurisdictions call together the legislature or parliament when there is a crisis; but the B.C. legislature had to be shut down because "reason must prevail". A few days before refusing a meeting with the Solidarity Coalition, Bennett claimed he wanted to "provide one more opportunity for groups and individuals to consult with ministers responsible for specific legislation that has been introduced but has not been passed." This included legislation dealing with the Rentalsman and human rights.

Although Bill 3 had passed, Bennett pointed out that "the opportunity does exist for the BCGEU, as it does for other public-sector unions, to negotiate ... their own contract language to govern layoffs and give exemptions from Bill 3." This was equivalent to showing a man a cliff and asking if he would rather jump or be pushed.

There was a mild aroma of bananas in the moist air of the Republic of British Columbia that evening.

The following day, as the lieutenant-governor proclaimed a handful of legislation and the House shut down for Bennett's "cooling-off period", the trade-union movement turned up the heat. Since mid-September, the Public-Sector Disputes and Strategy Committee of Operation Solidarity had been hunkered down, trying to figure what would take them beyond one demonstration after another. What emerged was a plan for an escalating general strike that kicked off on November 1 with the BCGEU and could put 200,000 public-sector workers on the street by November 15, less than four weeks away. The trigger for any action would be the final firing notice for the 1,600 public servants on Bill Bennett's hit list. A general strike had been muttered about unofficially since the beginning of the battle on July 7, and the committee's deliberations had led union leaders to the conclusion that a general strike was virtually inevitable; now they merely decided to draw out the process, rather than go off in one big bang.

What Operation Solidarity's head man Art Kube made clear in mid-October would become the most frequently forgotten fact in the whole dispute. The escalating strike was to concern itself with labour issues only. Kube was quite specific: "There's a principle involved. You don't fire people without regard to their collective agreement. If the BCGEU is successful in negotiating an exemption to Bill 3, that will set a plateau for every public-sector union in the province. This is everybody's fight." He did not talk about tenants' rights or human rights or the original Solidarity demands that all twenty-six pieces of legislation be withdrawn.

The final battle plan would be released following a critical strike co-ordinating meeting called by Operation Solidarity for October 31, the day before the threatened BCGEU shutdown. Kube's second-in-command Mike Kramer, pointed out that the public-sector unions were not alone. During the past week telegrams of support had come in from private-sector unions, including the Steelworkers in Trail. They would gladly come on board for any prolonged all-out action. "That," said Kramer, "is as close to a general strike as damn is to swearing."

October 22, the morning following the "indefinite" shutdown of the legislature, about three hundred members of the community groups in the Solidarity Coalition parked their cars and vans in axle-deep mud at the King Edward Campus of Vancouver City College at China Creek. They scraped their boots off on the threshold and filed into the antiseptic but charmingly new amphitheatre for the first province-wide meeting of the coalition. There was all the euphoria of a Woodstock concert, with up-country back-to-the-landers and radical feminists stoned on the prospect of fighting a great battle against an evil foe.

"There was sort of an aura going around," Renate Shearer remembered. "People walking around with books in their hands saying Winnipeg 1919, General Strike . . . .

[then there were] some religious people that were involved.
. . . A strike, a political protest, was not in their experience
and they were getting very, very uncomfortable." But
whatever discomfort there was was drowned out in the
psychedelic rhetoric of revolution.

Art Kube's opening address told the militants in the
crowd everything they feared, everything they didn't want
to hear. "Art said over and over again that if there is a strike,
the issues on the table will be Bill 2 and 3," Shearer insisted.
"He said that over and over again." The militants were in a
state of shock.

Frances Wasserlein of Women Against the Budget got to
her feet demanding that Kube say it wasn't so.

> I don't know when I've ever had a harder time in a
> political place than in that place . . . . Being astute pol-
> iticians ourselves, as women activists, we knew that
> something was coming that was going to be bad . . . .
> Several of us stood up in the general assemblies of that
> meeting and said: "Look, community groups are really
> worried that you guys are going to sell us out to get
> yourselves off the hook on Bill 3, and the concerns of
> the people who are not unionized, who are poor, who
> are women, who are gay, who are disabled, are going to
> go by the boards in order for the trade unions to protect
> their position. And tell us that you're not." And so they
> did. They told us they wouldn't.

Most of the crowd, including Wasserlein, suffered from
collective deafness: they had come so far, their cause was so
just, that they simply refused to believe – or even hear –
what Kube was saying. Later in the conference the Solidarity Coalition passed a motion calling for job action "up
to and including a general strike" to force the "repeal of the
entire legislative package and restoration of social
services".

The insecurity cut both ways. Kube had come up with the
idea of community groups and unions formally banding
together to fight the government legislation, but there was

tension from the beginning. Trade unions are clearly organized structures with elected officers, constitutions, and fixed memberships. The community groups were, for the most part, loose and organic. They decided things "collectively". There was no list that said, for example, "The following people constitute the full and complete membership of Women Against the Budget."

There had already been splits over the demonstration at Grace McCarthy's, the cabinet-office sit-in, and the huge petition campaign. Thousands of hours were spent by hundreds of people to gather thousands of names on a petition that was never presented to anybody. The militants and many of the community groups figured it was a waste of time from the start.

With the November 1 strike date just a week away, private-sector trade unionists like Jack Munro were beside themselves with rage: these community organizations were presuming to tell trade unionists what to do. Paying lip-service to feminist causes or human-rights issues was one thing; sharing power with these people was something else.

Munro was negotiating a new contract for the IWA, but other trade-union leaders convinced him he should find out what the Solidarity Coalition and the community groups were all about. After all, he was the BCFed's first vice-president, and the BCFed was bankrolling most of this operation. He attended "one meeting with all the goddamned bullshit" and came away with these thoughts:

> The Bennett government created the climate to put together a whole raft of groups of people who never, ever really had the ability to get together before. These groups of people all of sudden find this fantastic power where people are talking about strikes in the public sector and general strikes in the private sector and all this. Shit, they thought, this is fuckin' great. The same people who had never ever in their goddamned life . . . ever thought that they would sit down at an executive board and make these kinds of decisions. Like, where

the hell would you ever get enough people to attend the
Rural Lesbians' Association fuckin' meeting . . . sitting
next to the Gay Alliance, sitting next to the Urban
fuckin' Lesbians, and all this horseshit that goes on in
this fuckin' world these days, making a decision to
shut the province down. It was great. Trade unionists
. . . we were the turkeys in the goddamned thing.
Chicken-shit trade unionists. You could feel that we
were the goddamned moderates, for Christ's sake. I
should have been for all of these causes, a lot of causes
that I don't goddamned well agree with. I should have
been asking our people, who maybe were going into a
strike situation of our own, to come off the job. Well
that isn't the way the real world works.

People got caught up in this . . . . My cause is up at the
forefront. Jesus, fifty-five thousand or sixty thousand
people at Empire Stadium and fifty thousand people
marching around the hotel . . . . Certainly I was ex-
cited, no question about it. I think those were fantastic
demonstrations, and I don't know what we would ever
do again to get that kind of a demonstration other than
a peace march or something. But when it came to people drunk with this stance that we were going to shut
the province down and overthrow the government or
have this general strike, I don't know what they
thought was at the end of it if it wasn't to overthrow
the government. That's when I started to get pretty
goddamned nervous about what was happening.

By the end of October Jack Munro was sharing his nerv-
ousness with Jim Matkin, head of the Employers' Council.
Matkin, the father of the wage-restraint program and the
man who had been wet-nurse to three successive B.C. ministers of labour, had a network monitoring the rumble that
was building in the streets. He was regularly in contact with
Norman Spector, sporadically with Bill Bennett. Matkin
met a few times privately with Art Kube to try to convince
him that his social crusade was a mistake. He would wonder aloud whether Solidarity was a "new political party" or

"a monster out of control". While Spector continued to try to split the trade unions away from the community groups through a separate deal on Bill 3, Kube was trying to find some way of reaching Bennett and his cabinet for a way out. He enlisted the help of ex-Liberal MLA and radio talk-show host Barry Clark to make some approaches to the Liberal wing of cabinet. Clark came up empty.

When Bennett shut down the house on October 21, negotiations with the 45,000-member Government Employees' Union hadn't budged since they were formally started up on October 3. The union was taking its strike vote, the membership freaked out by on-again, off-again termination notices: the six hundred or so fired people in Human Resources were sent offers of redeployment and told to return to their original jobs. Then the redeployment plan was put on hold. Three of the human-rights workers who were dumped and declared redundant in July were receiving "merit pay" increases with their pay packets while they sat at home. Comic relief.

The BCGEU bargaining committee decided to apply a little pressure. The government negotiator, Mike Davison, didn't seem to have whole lot to say, so they hauled the government up in front of the Labour Relations Board for bargaining in bad faith. On October 24, special mediator Vince Ready was assigned to the dispute, and the negotiation session moved from Victoria to the Labour Relations Board's Vancouver offices overlooking False Creek. On October 27 the BCGEU announced the results of their strike vote: they had a clear mandate to hit the bricks. There was never any doubt.

Bill Bennett dispatched Norman Spector to negotiate for the government side; Cliff Andstein squared off for the union. It was time to get serious: the strike was four days away. One week later 28,000 teachers plus CUPE public-school support staff, community college faculty members, and university teachers were scheduled to walk – 80,000 workers in all.

Spector elbowed Mike Davison out of the way, and they got down to dealing with issues, not money. Money wasn't an immediate problem. The main issues were those 1,600 government workers, seniority provisions, and just how the government was planning to shrink or eliminate government programs.

By this time, Operation Solidarity was meeting daily for breakfast at the Sheraton Villa in Burnaby. The original escalating strike agenda was revised and revised again as union leaders jostled for advantage or got cold feet and figured their workers weren't going to go out. The Office and Technical Employees' Union seemed to be having some problems. Mike Kramer, the brassy secretary-treasurer of the BCFed, roared at anyone who came near his cage. Once the strike begins, he growled, "the ante will go up" to include the full goals of the Solidarity Coalition: the reinstatement of social services and human rights. Kramer was giving Kube a headache. Besides, relations with the NDP caucus were strained and worsening. Solidarity was getting all the headlines.

At the end of September Art Kube sold his executive on the idea of putting out a weekly newspaper: *The Solidarity Times*. Operation Solidarity kicked in $45,000 and hired Stan Persky, a Yippie socialist, as editor. Persky collected a small band of east-end, punkoid, anarchist writers, thrilled at the prospect of a regular paycheque, to chronicle the course of the revolution.

The first issue hit the streets along with the 50,000 demonstrators at the Socred convention; the second issue came a week later. The third issue of the paper was to appear as the BCGEU strike drew near. Persky and the kids decided to give their readers some history of the general strike in Canada and the possibility of a general strike in B.C. Persky assigned an energetic cub reporter to the legislature to interview NDP MLAS on the question: "What do you think of a general strike?" The unanimous answer was: "It sucks." Great story.

The morning the paper was going to press Persky was on the phone to his contact at Operation Solidarity, chief flak Gerry Scott. One of the best political organizers in the province, Scott was paid to smell trouble. Persky read the story to him, and Scott had a sinus attack. Three hours later Persky was at College Printers laying out the paper when he got a phone call. It was a conference call with Art Kube, Renate Shearer, Gerry Scott, and BCFed executive member Joy Langan, all sounding like they were shouting down a urinal. "Hi, Stan. This is Art, Renate, Gerry, and Joy calling. Hear you've got a story about the general strike. Well, we thought that it might not look so good if Operation Solidarity is planning a strike and the NDP MLAS say it sucks. See what we mean, Stan boy? Right." Persky was convinced to water down the story until it practically dribbled off the page.

On October 31, the afternoon before the BCGEU was going to walk, Bill Bennett went on television again. Negotiations that had been moving ahead four days earlier were now stalled. Norman Spector and his number-two man, Bob Plecas, were back in Victoria to brief the cabinet. But the B.C. Ferry and Marine Workers' Union had just quietly signed a deal with the government: a three-year contract with zip in the first year and, more important, an exemption to the firing provisions in Bill 3.

Bennett was on television to show the world how his legislation could work: all you needed was reasonable trade-union leaders. He wanted the BCGEU to call off its strike. If they did, he would send his negotiators back in and delay, for at least another two days, the firing of those 1,600 government workers. He had barely finished his statement and the TV lights were starting to cool, when he backed off. Negotiations would continue, he said, and the firings would be postponed, strike or no strike. Newspaper editorials called it an "olive branch".

At midnight, the strike began and government services ended. Liquor stores, the legislature, and provincial courts were all behind picket lines.

Once the BCGEU was on the street, meetings were begun to cut a deal for the teachers. Their strike vote was fairly soft – 59 per cent in favour. These people do not think of themselves as trade unionists, and most people in the union movement figured there was no way the teachers could pull

off a successful strike with that vote. But ever since the
start of Bill Bennett's restraint crusade back in 1982, teachers and school boards had been battered regularly. There
had been constant confusion and adjustments over budgets; class size had gone up; professional development days
had disappeared for a while. There were threats of firings;
curricula were jerked around, and teaching supplies
dwindled. Then came July 7. Teachers' seniority rights
under section 153 of the Public School Act were wiped out
by Bill 3. And there was some question whether they could
work out an exemption. A teacher walkout would not be
pleasant.

Sunday, November 6. Three days before teachers were
supposed to join the BCGEU workers on the picket line, B.C.
Teachers' Federation President Larry Kuehn joined Art
Kube, Jack Munro, and Jim Matkin in the offices of Ed
Peck, the bureaucrat who rules whether deals are accept-
able under Bill 3. Matkin had been on the blower to Bennett; Bennett didn't want a general strike. Matkin figured
there was a deal to be made. The idea was to work out the
wording for firings in the school system and to try and get
one school board and their teachers to accept the proposal.
Matkin said they came within inches of cutting a deal, but
Kuehn balked. He wanted guarantees that funding to the
education system would be restored. Matkin and Munro
hit the roof. Kuehn walked out, and Kube followed.

There was one last hope – the North Vancouver school
board. A sub-committee of that board and their teachers
had worked out a possible wording for an exemption to Bill
3. If the board accepted it, that would be the pattern to be
used province-wide. The next morning the deal went to the
North Vancouver board, as did a phone call from the deputy minister of education. He convinced the board that
they should dump the deal, and the minister of education,
Jack Heinrich, went on the tube to tell the province's teachers that what they were contemplating was illegal. They
could lose their teaching certificates.

If teachers weren't angry with the government before,
Heinrich's statement put them over the top. Just before six

that evening Kuehn announced that the teachers' strike was on. A brochure from BCTF headquarters, entitled "Why Teachers Are on Strike", listed among their demands: "restoration of social, democratic and human rights for all British Columbians; school services to be maintained at least at their present level over the next three years; and access to post-secondary education for all qualified students." This was considerably more than the basic labour issues of Bill 2 and Bill 3 that Kube and Operation Solidarity had announced a few weeks earlier.

School boards across the province attempted to block the strike with injunctions. Kim Campbell, chairman of the Vancouver school board and unsuccessful Socred candidate in the May 5 election, said teachers needed a "kick in the ass" and then muttered something about "terrorists holding us all for ransom".

By 2:00 A.M. the next morning the Fishermen's Union's George Hewison was yarded out of a deep sleep by the phone. It was from the war room in the basement of the B.C. Teachers' Federation Building on Burrard. They had news for George, and for his wife, Sherry Hillman, who was with Women Against the Budget and chairperson of the Lower Mainland Solidarity Coalition (which replaced the Lower Mainland Budget Coalition): the Vancouver school board had got its injunction just before midnight. The teachers couldn't be forced to come to class, but they were prohibited by law from picketing. They needed volunteers.

By 5:00 A.M. a long line of cars was moving slowly through the morning drizzle into the parking lot behind the BCGEU building on Canada Way; close to five hundred people were picking up picket signs. Building Trades unionists, Women Against the Budget, human-rights advocates, tenants – the lot. By six o'clock that morning every school in the city was covered.

Over 95 per cent of the province's teachers were off the job. The trade-union movement was as surprised as the Socreds; both had figured the teachers would fold. They didn't.

That night Art Kube addressed a Solidarity meeting in

New Westminster. He looked like a beaten man. In the middle of a halting speech, Kube wept; tears began to run down his puffy face. After weeks of endless meetings and building pressure, the man who had masterminded the Solidarity movement was falling apart. As the strike deadline drew near, Kube was becoming increasingly isolated – partly because he wouldn't share responsibility with Operation Solidarity and partly because people such as Jack Munro were telling him he was nuts to take the province into a general strike. With faltering internal political support and failing health, Kube collapsed. He was shipped home to bed. His old phone was disconnected, and an unlisted line was installed. Norman Spector said Kube had lost his nerve.

The next few days were a blur. Some of the key players – Larry Kuehn, Mike Kramer, Norman Spector, Jack Munro – attended meetings that ended only so they could attend other meetings. Accounts of where those meetings were, on what day, who was at them, exactly what was decided under the pressure of a building strike and impending deadlines are often at variance. But from a fairly careful gleaning of documents and participants' memories a scenario emerges.

The morning following the teachers' walk-out, the Operation Solidarity meeting at the Sheraton Villa went on for five hours. Now that Kube was out of the way, Kramer and Munro took charge. They were trying to hammer out a deal to offer to Bennett. Kube was called from time to time for comments. The members were getting skittish. The leaders were getting skittish. Everything was solid on the picket lines, but the number of calls to BCFed headquarters demanding an end to the escalating strike was increasing. They wanted to get out while they could.

Of course this was not what was being served up for public consumption. Private-sector union leaders, including Jack Munro and Telecommunications Workers Union president Bill Clark, were thundering that their members were ready to join their public-sector brothers and sisters on the streets. Munro said, "I'm extremely upset by the hawks [in the Socred cabinet], and I guess if they want war we're going to give them war." Mike Kramer was equally bellicose. Now that injunctions against picketing were starting to flood out of the Labour Relations Board hearing rooms, Kramer snarled, "If there is one move against any one of us, we will retaliate, and I mean massive retaliation . . . an all-out war."

The breakfast meeting at the Villa came up with a five-point program, an opening gambit that included Bill 3 exemptions for all public-sector unions: education financing maintained at 1983 levels; changes to the human-rights and landlord-tenant legislation; and consultation on social issues. An earlier meeting of a few heavies on the BCFed executive decided that Munro would do all the negotiating. Kramer would be the sidekick.

Munro got hold of Matkin, who was doing legwork for Bennett and reporting through Spector. Munro, Kramer, and Matkin met on Thursday, November 10: Munro pitched the deal and they kicked it around. Matkin said he'd pass the offer on to Spector, who was still at the Labour Relations Board negotiating with the BCGEU.

The next day Munro and Kramer pulled into the underground parking lot at the Labour Relations Board and headed up to the third floor, unnoticed by the reporters camped out in the second-floor reception area, monitoring the BCGEU talks. Munro arrived first. Kramer drifted up to the third floor looking for LRB chairman Stephen Kelleher and walked out of the elevator smack into the middle of a screaming brawl. Cliff Andstein and BCGEU president Norm Richards were taking on Jack Munro. Andstein was wearing a bit thin: there was round-the-clock negotiating, his family was under police protection after repeated phone threats to his wife that she'd never live to see a collective agreement, and a few of the BCGEU offices in the Cariboo had been shot up. Andstein overheard Munro talking about the BCGEU collective agreement. He was already aware of Munro's pressure on the BCGEU to get a quick settlement. There was a lot of: "You stay out of our fucking negotiations. We don't interfere in your fucking negotiations" before things calmed down. As Andstein and Richards left, Spector slipped through the reception area, stepping over reporters' bodies, wincing in the pungent atmosphere of too many cigarettes and not enough showers, and slipped upstairs for the first in a series of secret meetings with Munro, Kramer, and Kelleher.

The meetings began with Kramer and Munro huffing and puffing while Norman told them that their whole strike was on the verge of collapse. He couldn't promise them anything definite, he said, but they could come to a general understanding; then Munro would have to fly up to Kelowna and meet with the premier. (The decision to send Munro to Kelowna to represent Operation Solidarity was made by the BCFed executive for two reasons: they wanted Bennett involved in any settlement because they didn't trust a deal with Spector alone. They also knew that the coalition would accuse them of selling out the community groups when the deal went down and figured that Munro could take the heat.)

The Labour Relations Board was a three-ring circus. The BCGEU negotiations were going on at one end of the second floor. The meeting rooms at the other end of the second floor were full of community-college management and their lawyers trying to get injunctions to stop picketing by the union types and their lawyers sitting across the table from them. On the third floor, there were the secret meetings. Everywhere else was the press, filling all the available floor space, drinking coffee, smoking cigarettes, and swapping lies.

Bill Bennett was having quite a different day. He was at home in Kelowna, his refuge. That morning BCTV's Pamela Martin had turned up with a crew to start shooting a documentary on Bill Bennett after ten years in elected office. Pamela, Bill, and the crew hopped into a car for a half hour drive off into the bush to John Ritchie's cabin. Ritchie is a boyhood buddy of Bill's, who dropped out of the family auction business a few years back and moved with his wife onto a little ranch with a log cabin and a wood stove.

John rustled up some of his organic home-made muffins

and coffee for the folks. Then Bill and John and Dick Stewart, Bill's old pal and tennis partner, sat down for a little game of crib. The boys at play. Roll those cameras. When the coffee and muffins were done, John had the horses saddled. Bill climbed on a sixteen-hands-high chestnut with a white blaze on its forehead; they put Pamela up on a pinto. And with Dick and John they headed out for a ride. Nobody talked politics. It was part of the deal.

John was in the lead when they came to a fork in the trail. They could either go up a steep bank and over a ridge or go around it. John headed straight up. Bill started up, but his horse stumbled into the hill. Down at the bottom, Dick yelled up to him not to bother. Up on the ridge, John was saying the same thing. Bill kicked the big chestnut on again, and again it stumbled into the hill, pinning Bill's leg. More shouting. Again he kicked the horse on, and a third time it stumbled. Pamela figured he was out to kill himself. On the fourth try, the horse finally made it up the ridge. Then it was all laughing and scratching, like a bunch of kids who had double-dared each other, and they rode back to John's cabin.

When Pamela and the crew returned to Bennett's house early in the afternoon, Bill offered them coffee out of the big urn on the kitchen counter, served in Styrofoam cups. Then he was on the phone. In fact no sooner did he finish one call and get off the phone than it would ring again to shatter the Remembrance Day calm.

Norman Spector down in Vancouver wanted to apprise his boss of events as each meeting with Munro and Kramer took place and as the BCGEU negotiations progressed. The sticking point for Spector in his meetings with Munro and Kramer was the demand to maintain education funding levels. No way. On the other demands, Spector wasn't promising anything specific. In fact, no specific deal was reached in Vancouver, only an agenda for discussion between Munro and Bennett. Bennett agreed to meet with Munro in Kelowna after the BCGEU reached a tentative settlement with Spector.

Saturday afternoon, while Munro and Kramer were sitting in an ailing Art Kube's kitchen explaining the plan for a settlement, the Vancouver *Sun* broke the news about the secret meetings with Spector and the five-point Solidarity demand. People on the Solidarity Coalition steering committee went straight up a wall. They tracked Renate Shearer to a friend's retreat on Saltspring Island, but she didn't have any idea what was going on. Nobody had asked the community groups about a deal; nobody had asked her. Once Kube was out of it, all communications between Operation Solidarity and the Solidarity Coalition had dried up. The previous Thursday, Shearer had phoned around to find out if there could possibly be a settlement that weekend. She was told no. She needed a break and took it.

Saturday came and went, and the BCGEU negotiations still dragged, although pressure was building; the province's transportation systems would shut down at midnight on Sunday. As Sunday's dawn was coming up over the far end of False Creek, the BCGEU settlement began to fall into place. By early afternoon it was done. At 3:00 P.M. Spector said, "It demonstrates that any reduction in the workplace can take place in a fair, equitable, and hopefully sensitive manner." Andstein called it a "no-concession agreement". Cliff Andstein and Norm Richards walked down the hall to meet with their bargaining committee and join in a chorus of "Solidarity Forever".

Jack Munro grabbed his raincoat and found Gerry Scott and Norman Spector. They piled into Jack's 1980 Chrysler New Yorker, filling Scott in on the deal as they headed out to the South Terminal where a government Cessna Citation would fly them to Kelowna.

A cab took the trio out to Bennett's house with a media contingent bringing up the rear. They were met by Bill's son Kevin, and the Family's English sheepdog, Sherlock. Bennett greeted them near the door with, "Where's Art, Jack?"

Scott chatted with Audrey Bennett and the kid in the kitchen. Munro and Spector trudged across the indoor-outdoor carpet, past the recreation-room pool table and four spare tires leaning against the wall, and into the living room where Bennett had spent a relaxing afternoon in his rocker watching football on the tube. Munro took one couch, Spector the other. Audrey brought them cheese, crackers, antipasto, and mugs of coffee from the bottomless urn in the kitchen. It was 6:30 P.M.

Bennett started the discussion by asking Munro how many of his members were out of work these days, a reminder that private-sector union members were suffering more through the recession than their public-sector brothers, whom Munro was in Kelowna to represent. Then they went through the demands, with Spector playing interpreter. Bill 2, the legislation that would have gutted the BCGEU collective agreement, would die. In fact, it was a bill that was born to die. There was no need for it, now that the BCGEU had settled. Most of what they talked about was consultation on this and consultation on that. No commitments.

Then they got to the short strokes. Bennett said that education financing would not be maintained at 1983 levels; that teachers would not get a nickel of the $18 million or so that had been saved in forfeited teachers' wages because of the strike. He also said that because a couple of his ministers had been on his case about this meeting he wouldn't announce any deal that night; he wanted to discuss it with his cabinet first.

Jack Munro likes movie mogul Samuel Goldwyn's line: "A verbal agreement isn't worth the paper it's written on." As he sat in Bennett's living room he could see the pickle he was in. He got up and headed upstairs, where Scott joined him in Bennett's French-blue bedroom. Before he picked up the phone on the mahogany bedside table, he brought Scott up to date. Scott was not very happy and told Munro he was in real trouble. Munro phoned Kube at home and got more of the same. "Forget it," Kube said. "Get the hell out of there." Munro refused: "I'm not leaving here without an agreement."

While Munro and Bennett were sitting down to talk, members of the Operation Solidarity steering committee were joined by Renate Shearer and B.C. Teachers' Federation president Larry Kuehn in the boardroom at the BCGEU

office in Burnaby. They were waiting for word from Kelowna. By the time Munro hung up on his call to Kube and
placed his first call to Kramer at BCGEU headquarters you
could hear laughs, cheers, and the popping of corks. The
strategy had been to keep all the picket lines up until there
was a settlement on the Operation Solidarity demands, but
the strike was over for the BCGEU bargaining team and they
were partying.

Munro told Kramer about the heat Bennett was getting
from his cabinet ministers and that there was no way the
$18 million was going to go back into the education system
if it was going to be used for wages or pay increases for
teachers. Kramer told Munro to go back and try again for
the education money. Then Kramer returned to the Operation Solidarity meeting and ran the deal past them. Kuehn
wanted assurances that money would be spent in the education system.

While Munro was on the phone, Spector told Bennett
how badly Operation Solidarity wanted out of the mess
they had created by an escalating strike. They would accept
his revised demands. The strike was collapsing; by the
middle of the week fifty-five school districts would have
injunctions against picketing. When Munro came back to
nail things down on that extra money and the teachers,
Bennett just sat there. Then he asked Jack about his garden-
ing. The discussion was over.

Munro trudged back upstairs and phoned Kramer again.
Kramer agreed that they had got everything they could get,
which wasn't a hell of a lot.

Munro and Scott went back to the living room for a half-
hour of chit-chat with Spector and Bennett – the game,
horseback riding with Pamela Martin – while they waited
for Kramer to talk the deal over with the Operation Solidarity committee. The deal was passed, but not unan-
imously. Munro phoned Kube, who was now ready to buy
the deal. The Kelowna Accord was on.

There was no agreement on human rights legislation or
the Rentalsman. There was no commitment to maintaining

education funding levels, just a promise to consult. The strike would be called off.

Bennett and Munro stepped out onto the back patio and into the glare of the TV lights just before 10:30 P.M. All Bennett would say was that they had reached "an avenue for resolving the difficulties". He refused to discuss specifics, but there would be "meaningful consultation".

Back in Burnaby, Renate Shearer couldn't face the Solidarity Coalition meeting waiting for her at their West Broadway offices. None of the community issues had been dealt with, yet the strike had been called off. Kramer asked two union leaders, Leif Hansen of the meatcutters' local and BCFed executive member Joy Langan, to go along with Renate and explain the deal. The meeting started before 10:00 P.M.; it was loud and acrimonious. All the confusion of the past weeks and months over why there was a strike, what the issues were, and who was making the decisions poured out all over again. Kramer cruised by after midnight in a belligerent and abusive mood. He dumped on the coalition. They had no right to tell the trade-union movement when to go on strike and when to call it off. "It was a terrible night," that went on to something like two o'clock in the morning, Shearer remembers. "People believed and they cared and they were desperate, and everything we had come together for was still up in the air."

Early Monday morning some 250 Solidarity union leaders met in Burnaby to hear the details of the agreement. Most of them figured that they had got the best they could in the circumstances. They committed another $50,000 to a Solidarity war chest. That night Kramer and Kube turned up at a meeting of the Lower Mainland Solidarity Coalition at the Fishermen's Hall. The coalition booed Kube and hurled abuse at him. They wanted to know why they hadn't been consulted as part of the Sunday deal. They said they had been sold out. Kube and Kramer fled the meeting and headed into the evening downpour.

11
THE NEW REALITY

Solidarity and the trade-union movement were really beaten at the Expo 86 site. Not somewhere off in the boonies, not in some back-alley scrap or some living-room summit, but right out in the open and smack in the middle of Bill Bennett's proudest megaproject, the development he likes to call "downtown British Columbia". At Expo the Tough Guy pulled off the biggest power-grab trade unions had experienced in a decade. It was neo-conservative restraint at work in the private sector. Bill Bennett was putting into practice the ideas about reducing "pass-through costs" that had been discussed at the Okanagan Lake retreat after the 1983 election. He stripped power from the special-interest group that most regularly and vocally threatened an era he referred to now as the New Reality and gave that power to the right-to-work crowd, that small but aggressive band of non-union contractors from the Socred heartland, the Fraser Valley Bible Belt.

At 6:30 on Monday morning, March 19, 1984, the sun cracked over the Granville Bridge, sliced through the overcast, and glanced off the twenty-storey crane at the Pennyfarthing construction site on the south shore of False Creek, the latest battleground in the union/non-union war. The sign on the crane's crossbar had been disfigured early in this bitter confrontation. "KERKHOFF", the notorious non-union contractor's name, had been altered to "JERK

OFF". Just the night before a Solidarity banner had been raised above the name.

At the chain-link gates men in their peaked caps, rough jackets, and steel-toed boots gathered around barrels of burning trash for another day of waiting. They were, for the most part, members of the building trades unions. Unemployed.

When they raised their eyes to the horizon, every tower of offices or apartments they saw on the skyline from the creek to the North Shore mountains had been built by union labour. These men were on the burning edge of a radical change, a change that was hitting all of western Canada where, until recently, the construction unions had had a virtual lock on all major projects beyond residential construction. The change was forced by the recession. Massive unemployment made union members more willing to put their union card in their boot, take a walk over to a non-union job site, and work for a third less. In British Columbia the unemployment rate in the building trades was well over 50 per cent.

In 1976, as soon as Bill Bennett took power, he killed a piece of NDP legislation that made it mandatory for all government construction to be performed by union contractors and union crews. But nothing of significance changed for the next six years. Non-union firms dominated the housing market and, as the recession deepened, made slow inroads into commercial construction projects. Then, in 1982, the government awarded a large contract for a new provincial courthouse building in Kamloops to J.C. Kerkhoff and Sons Construction Ltd.

The head of that firm is Bill Kerkhoff, a tall, slim, thirty-seven-year-old father of six, who still speaks with a clipped Dutch accent more than twenty years after he immigrated with his family to the Fraser Valley and the welcoming Dutch Reformed Church community at Chilliwack. He soon found work with a local labour contractor. By the time he was twenty he was running his own construction business with his father and his older brother, Casey. In 1975 he

picked up his first big contract, a $400,000 plant west of
Chilliwack in Langley, and had his first run-in with trade
unions. He sub-contracted to union and non-union firms
alike and ran into the Building Trades Council's long-
standing non-affiliation clause. (That clause states that a
union worker can refuse to work on the same site as a non-
union worker.) This landed Kerkhoff before the Labour
Relations Board for the first time and convinced him "only
to work with non-union people. It wasn't that we didn't
want to deal with the unions, but they didn't want to deal
with us." Nothing has changed since then.

It is still unclear just how Bill Kerkhoff hustled his way
into the Pennyfarthing construction project. The first
phase of these luxury condominiums was built by a union
contractor, Stevenson Construction Ltd., owned by a partner in Pennyfarthing. Stevenson's men were putting in the
footings for phase two when Kerkhoff turned up at a Pennyfarthing meeting and convinced the board of directors to
let him bid on the unfinished work. Kerkhoff came in close
to $2 million under the union contract figure from Steven-
son and was the only other contractor asked to bid. The
financial institution backing the project, the B.C. Central
Credit Union, was put under enormous pressure by the
trade-union movement to block the deal. There was a series
of negotiating sessions to try to pare down the union contract price. They whittled the difference to $700,000 be-
fore the talks collapsed.

Kerkhoff was awarded the contract in early March; the
pickets went up on March 5. Men began to spend their days
at the Pennyfarthing site instead of at union hiring halls, at
home in front of the tube, or in the pub.

A fifty-year-old operating engineer sits on a stump in front
of the main gate and warms himself by the fires burning in
two rusted five-gallon drums stuffed with cedar. "We
shouldn't have backed off when we had those bastards on
the run last November." Solidarity. The general strike that
never was. The man has worked seven shifts in the past year
and a half.

Just eighteen days ago this was a union site; now these men have no legal right to be here, to congregate, to mill about, to picket, to protest. Eight days ago the Labour Relations Board ruled against them. A fifty-two-year-old carpenter sucks on a smoke and barks, "If they bust it here, it'll all go down the toilet. I'll be working for ten dollars or twelve dollars an hour." He hasn't worked for a year.

By 8:20 A.M. the blessed coffee wagon arrives. Gallons of hot liquid and dozens of sticky, sweet buns are disgorged from its quilted, stainless-steel body.

The previous Saturday the Building Trades leader, Roy Gauthier, spoke at a rally here and was full of tough talk. Anyone who wanted to build a project non-union would pay a heavy price. "I think we've got to convince Bennett that we can screw up Expo 86," he said as he looked across False Creek to the 156-acre site for the exposition. Expo 86 is the promise all these men have waited for; it is the dream that has warmed them during their endless months on unemployment insurance and welfare. Now they see it all being blown away in a non-union hurricane.

By 10:30, non-union sub-contractor Ewald Rempel rolls up to the site cool and calm in his new Ford Ranger, a change from the Rolls-Royce he usually drives. Rempel is leader of the province's right-to-work contractors and has been on the trade union's hit list for more than a decade.

Ewald Rempel use to pick tobacco on Sumas Prairie when he was a kid. He'll tell you that to persuade you he understands the working man. Now he owns the biggest ready-mix concrete company in B.C., which has the contract to supply cement to Pennyfarthing. From his headquarters in Abbotsford he controls a $25-million-a-year operation with 80 trucks and 150 employees. It has been built up during seventeen years by non-union labour. The Sandman Inn in Vancouver was Rempel's first big project; union members tried to stop it and failed. A dozen years ago the union movement branded his operation "unfair", and refused to supply his trucks with cement in Canada. Since then he has been hauling his loads from over the border.

Crossing a picket line does not break Ewald Rempel's

heart. He has come to the site to be provocative. Rempel and Kerkhoff want this project to start, but they need some legal muscle. That's what the provocation is about, and it works. Rempel's new truck is surrounded by angry picketers. First they rock it; then someone pulls out a set of keys and works away at the cream-and-green paint job. "SCAB" is scratched along one side. Another man slashes the tires with a knife. A third slices off tire valves. Then, from somewhere at the back of the growing crowd, a glob of foul-smelling organic crud comes flying through the air, splatters Rempel's door, and slops through the open window onto his shirt and trousers. People nearby turn their heads at the stench. Rempel calmly pulls himself out of the truck and makes his way to the back of the vehicle to check for damage. The police move in from their nearby observation points and escort him away as people downwind turn their heads and cover their mouths.

The picketers go back to their posts, their card games, and their conversations; the crowd seems to dwindle. It comes alive again just before 4:00 P.M. when a Kerkhoff Construction flatbed truck loaded with hoarding material pulls up at the site. It is surrounded. A front tire is flattened, and the air lines are cut. The back wheels are locked, and the fuel tank cap is ripped off. The truck limps away for half a dozen blocks, sloshing diesel and whatever the picketers have poured into the tank. The people inside the truck have made their point.

Within the week, B.C. Supreme Court Justice Allan McEachern forces the union and its members to back off. The project will be built non-union. "It worked basically the way we planned it," Bill Kerkhoff confesses. "We expected something like this to happen, and that's why we sent someone in right at the beginning to provoke it, if you like, because we wanted to have a confrontation right up front. We didn't want to get six months into the contract and have all this happen."

Ewald Rempel promotes the notion, increasingly popular in British Columbia, that unions have too much power. He has been campaigning for years to convince the Socred government to get rid of closed shops and make it easier for people like him and Bill Kerkhoff to operate. Bennett has resisted the annual call for the right-to-work legislation that would make it optional for a person to belong to a trade union in order to hold a job. That demand is made at every Socred convention. Rempel figures that the mood is about to change.

> I know that Bennett . . . doesn't want the right-to-work legislation. But you know how politicians are when it becomes politically opportune. He may move that way . . . . I think that Pennyfarthing has hurt the union cause immeasurably. Decent people don't go for these type of tactics, and the union bosses in B.C. are going to have to clean up their act. Their penetration is going to drop and drop and drop unless they change their tactics.

Roy Gauthier has good reason to believe that Pennyfarthing is just the opening skirmish. His talks with Expo Chairman Jimmy Pattison have not been going well. They began in 1982 when Pattison came out to see Gauthier at the Building Trades headquarters in Burnaby. They had three meetings based on the assumption that Expo would go all union. The discussions turned on Pattison's demand for a no-strike agreement; but Gauthier was cool to the idea. In September 1983 everything changed. The reason, Pattison bluntly points out, was simple: "What happened was that there was an election."

Jimmy Pattison has been running the Expo corporation since late 1980. Bennett was down in the Wall Street canyons fussing over British Columbia's latest bond issue when he offered Pattison the job. Jimmy took the call in his office in the Guinness Tower in Vancouver, the hub of his growing empire. Directly behind Jimmy's head was the only fixture attached to the walls of that room, a motto in an austere frame: "There is no limit to what a man can do or where he can go if he doesn't mind who gets the credit."

Jimmy Pattison has gone and done plenty. He's a kid

from Saskatchewan who moved to the east side of Vancouver, dropped out of a commerce degree at UBC, and started kicking tires and selling cars. He has moved up from the loud checkered polyester jackets, exotic ties, and white belts of the car lot to ultra-suede, but he is still a blue-eyed, freckle-faced speedball, although his red hair has been giving way to a rising forehead.

He is a workaholic. As he speaks on the phone he glances at his watches. The one on his right hand, a Piaget, is set for Vancouver. The Chopard on his left has two faces, one set for New York, the other for Geneva. In his pocket he carries a third timepiece, a tiny S.T. Dupont travel alarm. It is set for whatever time zone he finds himself in.

When he has time he goes to church at the Glad Tidings Temple. Jimmy is born again. He is reputed to have written out a $1 million cheque and slid it into the collection plate one Sunday just to give the temple's building fund a boost. He used to play the trumpet in the temple band, but he now does most of his playing on his eighty-five-foot motor yacht which has an organ and a piano. The man is teetotal and a fan of Premier Bill Bennett.

A local lefty once sidled up to Jimmy at a sip-and-shake government function and asked, "Just how right-wing are you?"

Jimmy quipped, "Why, I'm so right-wing I invited Alexander Haig to talk to the key executives of all my companies."

"My God," gasped the lefty, "you may as well have invited Idi Amin!"

"I didn't know he was available," Jimmy shot back.

By 1984 Jimmy was spending five days a week, from seven in the morning until after dark, toiling for free at his Expo office. He does his own wheeling and dealing of close to a billion dollars in annual sales on the weekends. His holdings include an airline, a radio station, a chain of supermarkets, and the sign company that owns that symbol of Canadian crass, the Honest Ed's eyesore at Bathurst and Bloor in Toronto. He also owns the magazine wholesaler that distributes most of the printed soft-core pornography in British Columbia – a source of some embarrassment but considerable income for Jimmy – and a finance company in Switzerland that he visits most weekends. The wad of bills in his pocket is held together by a money clip with the U.S. presidential seal, a gift from Gerry Ford. If you think Jimmy Pattison belongs in *Ripley's Believe It or Not*, you'll be happy to know that he owns that, too.

While Jimmy boasts that he, like the other people who sit on the Expo 86 board of directors, receives no money for his contribution to the fair, at least ten of Jimmy's companies have contracts with Expo. This is not seen as a conflict of interest by the Nouveau Socreds. The minister responsible for Expo, Claude Richmond, explains: "If we had not allowed some of these companies to do business with Expo, we probably would have lost the benefit of these people on the board."

The legend of Jimmy Pattison's toughness began back in his early car-dealing days – at the end of each month, he fired the salesman with the lowest sales – but there are moments when he can be a shade less ruthless. Take, for example, Expo and the Mercedes sedan. On two consecutive days in August 1983 Jimmy pulled into his Expo parking stall at the Scotia Tower in Vancouver and noticed a sparkling new blue Mercedes 300sD in the Expo stall next to his. Finally he could contain his curiosity no longer and asked his vice-president of finance who owned the fancy hunk of iron. The word came back that the car was owned by Expo. It was purchased by Expo's new chief executive officer, Mike Bartlett, the man whom Pattison hired away from Canada's Wonderland in Ontario after rejecting 112 unacceptable applicants. Jimmy's reaction was immediate. "Get that car out of here. We will sell it right now." With the government cutting back on education, health care, legal aid, and paper clips, you don't waltz around in a Crown-owned Mercedes. The car was put up for tender.

At the next board meeting two bids were discussed. One was from Mercedes of Canada for about $32,000; the second was from Jim Pattison Leasing for $48,267. Jimmy declared his conflict of interest and then bought the car, which he later unloaded for $41,000 and absorbed the loss. (Bartlett drove a more modest leased vehicle until complaints about his profligacy and his abrasive management style combined with a leak of the Mercedes story two years later. In June 1985 he was fired.)

In September 1983 the fifteen-person Expo board met at the Expo construction office, an old brick building on Mainland Street. The purpose of the meeting was to reconsider whether the fair should be built exclusively by union labour. The reasoning went something like this: if we want to ensure that the project gets done on time with the least possibility of labour disruptions we should cut a deal with Roy Gauthier and the Building Trades Council. They give us a no-strike agreement like Wacky got when he built the Peace River power project, and we have no problem with their non-affiliation clause. Our technical people figure that non-union contractors don't have the expertise to pull it off, anyway. An open site with union and non-union will just create a war, and wars cost money and time. The vote was fourteen to one in favour of a union solution. The dissenting vote was that of Claude Richmond, the Socred minister of tourism.

Ten days later Richmond was back at the Expo board. Bill Bennett was insisting that Expo be an open site. Union and non-union outfits would be allowed to bid, and the lowest bidder would get the contract. The Expo board was put off by Bennett's cavalier interference, especially since he had been telling the world that Expo decisions were not being tampered with politically.

Meetings continued between Pattison and Gauthier through the fall. The meetings were infrequent and difficult. The province and the labour movement were preoccupied with Solidarity street protests, closure in the legislature, and strikes in the public service. The few contracts for preliminary work let at Expo were, coincidentally, given to union firms.

By spring 1984 the B.C. labour scene was still in a mess. In the private sector, the IWA had settled on a three-year deal.

The alliance they had forged with the province's two pulp unions when they started talks with the industry was in tatters, and the pulp unions were demanding more than Jack Munro had been able to secure for his IWA members. The pulp companies figured their best strategy was a lockout. The pulp workers across the province threw up picket lines not just at their own mills but also at IWA operations – secondary picketing. Jack Munro frothed at the mouth. He had never been on the best of terms with the pulp unions – in 1975, when the NDP government ordered the IWA and the pulp workers back to work, Jack went along willingly, but the pulp-union leadership blasted Dave Barrett.

Munro called the secondary pickets "immoral", even though he had pioneered the tactic in B.C. The IWA was suffering close to 40 per cent unemployment among its members. Munro's members were getting into brawls with pulp picketers; nobody wanted to miss another paycheque. He sympathized with IWA workers who crossed the line. Meanwhile the Building Trades were waging war on Bill Kerkhoff at the Pennyfarthing site. It was not an inspiration to all the foreign investment that Bill Bennett said was just off shore waiting.

Bill Bennett was polling. In January Decima Research told the Expo board that 87 per cent of British Columbians supported the decision to hold Expo in B.C.; 91 per cent believed that Expo would have a positive impact on job creation. A related survey by Market Facts of Canada projected a potential attendance for Expo 86 of 20- to 28-million visitors, assuming each Vancouver resident attended the fair 6.6 times.

As British Columbians watched Ewald Rempel having his tires slashed on the TV evening news, Allan Gregg's little telephone warriors were asking a scientifically selected number of B.C. households if they thought unions had too much power. While IWA members were screaming at their pulp-worker brothers to get the hell out, the pollsters were asking: What do you think of secondary picketing? The answers reinforced a view that the unions were not popular institutions.

The data was faithfully fed to Bill Bennett, and a careful and crafty plot hatched in his bellicose mind. Typically he proceeded to locate, isolate, and destroy – or at least maim – his enemy. On March 19 Bill Bennett announced: "It would be a tragedy if people set out to sabotage Expo. I guess they'd have to explain to all the British Columbians who were going to get jobs why they did it." A dispute such as the one holding up the Pennyfarthing development would not simply delay Expo, "it would cancel it."

Ten days later, on March 29, Bill Bennett went on province-wide television. The legislature was not in session. (After the "indefinite" shutdown in October, it was opened and aired out for less than two weeks at the end of January and then shut down again.) He ordered the pulp industry to lift its lock-out. The pulpworkers were to drop their picket lines and go back to work. He gave Jimmy Pattison ten days to cut a deal with Gauthier; at the end of those ten days Pattison was to recommend the future of Expo.

"These are difficult economic times and new realities must take hold," Bennett said. "The growth of non-union firms is simply an example of the market in action – a gale of competition in a previously insulated environment . . . . The front-line mentality we witnessed last week at False Creek must be replaced by the bottom-line mentality, or jobs that are now on the drawing board will not materialize."

Then he crooned that popular neo-conservative theme: special-interest groups like unions are anti-democratic; they inhibit freedom and cause discrimination. "The bottom line is that there will be no discrimination in British Columbia based on union or non-union status." Unions insisting that their negotiated non-affiliation clauses be honoured were asking for "special treatment at the expense of others during times of recession".

Having created the crisis, Bennett once again left others to try and deal with it: "It would disturb me greatly," he said, "as I know it would disturb most British Columbians, if Expo had to be cancelled." Half the province was sent into frenzy. Town councils were in the middle of planning their Expo programs, land speculators were already spending profits from land they would soon sell or develop near the Expo site; people were lamenting Canada's tarnished reputation should the project be scrapped, and most cabbies and waitresses in the lower mainland were watching the evaporation of the first chunk of steady work they'd seen in years. Anti-union sentiment erupted from every corner of the land.

Pattison's meetings with Gauthier increased in number and length. They were held in secret, mostly in Pattison's offices in the Guinness Tower, which had a boardroom and kitchen facilities. The two men started in the morning and went all day and half the night. At times they were joined by Mike Bartlett or a few labour lawyers. Gauthier said that the construction unions would allow non-union companies to work at any Expo site provided they were paid union rates. He would guarantee a stoppage-free construction period if Expo management agreed to the condition.

The problem with the offer was that it failed to help the non-union firms who were to provide Bennett's "gale of competition". Most of their competitive edge came from lower wage rates. Besides, Bennett was trying to convince people that he would save great gobs of money by effectively destroying the non-affiliation clauses in union contracts. Bennett had people believing that the fair was having money problems, but Jimmy Pattison denied it: "It had nothing to do with saving money. It was a major philosophical change that we were going to have an open site in downtown Vancouver."

The cost estimates of the fair had rocketed all over the place since the project was first announced in 1978 as a 100th birthday present for Vancouver. Total costs began at $78 million. By 1980 the Socreds had released a "ballpark figure" of $137.85 million; the deficit for the 150-acre extravaganza would be $12 million minus whatever they could make selling stamps and coins. In March 1982, a month after Bennett started his restraint crusade, the estimated cost of the fair was up to $170 million.

By April 1982 Bennett was announcing: "Expo will stand on its own and even make a small surplus." The total cost of $367 million would be covered by gate receipts and $100 million from a lottery fund. "No tax dollars will be received [by Expo] from the provincial government either this year or any other year." He added proudly that the fair would generate $65 million in provincial taxes. When Jimmy Pattison handed in his final budget in 1983 the cost of the fair was up to $806 million. The deficit was $311 million. The province would kick in $250 million in lottery funds – up from $100 million – and the fair would generate $126 million in new tax revenue. (Expo and the government sat on those final figures for more than a year, until January 1985.)

On the morning of April 6, 1984, eight days after Bill Bennett's ultimatum on Expo, Pattison announced that he couldn't come to an agreement with Gauthier. Before seeing Bennett, he met with his board at 1000 Beach, the old Westinghouse building. The board moved in at 2:00 P.M. and all the Expo staff was blown out of the building by security people. The phones were taken off the hook, and a seven-hour discussion ensued.

Four days later Jimmy turned up in Victoria with his recommendations. The first one was to cancel the fair and cut the government's losses of $80 million. The second alternative, which didn't get any publicity at the time, was to go ahead with the fair only after bringing in some legislative muscle to strong-arm the unions. Bennett decided to go with the fair, naturally – just look at the polls. He would still like a deal, but he was prepared to tough it out. Just let the unions dare to screw things up.

He set his legislative draftsmen to finalizing the first major overhaul of the B.C. Labour Code since the NDP had been in power. On May 8, 1984, at 6:00 P.M., Bennett introduced the fruits of their labour. His timing was perfect. The new amendments fit the mood of the time, a mood he had helped to create. It would be more difficult for unions to organize and easier for workers to get rid of their union. Secondary picketing was virtually wiped out. Legal political strikes like those Solidarity had been pulling off a few months earlier were eliminated. Large building sites like Expo could be declared "special economic development projects" that would be immune from union non-affiliation clauses.

Two former Labour Relations Board chairmen joined the voices of labour protesting the legislation. From his office at Harvard, Paul Weiler said the amendments were too heavily weighted against labour unions and would encourage employer interference in union organizing drives. Don Munroe, a private arbitrator, said, "This is clear evidence that the government's philosophy in labour relations is to discourage any growth in collective bargaining." The legislation was passed but not proclaimed.

At the end of May 1984 the Expo board met to award two contracts. At the beginning of the meeting Pattison read a lengthy harangue against the board's pro-union tendencies. The screed was signed by Bill Kerkhoff. The second contract awarded that day went to a union firm; the first, for $4.4 million, went to J.C. Kerkhoff and Sons. Kerkhoff's bid was $45,000 lower than a union firm, Van Construction. If you figure that 35 per cent of the cost of construction is labour and that Kerkhoff had a 40 per cent break on wages over his union competitors, Van Construction would have had to dish out about $626,000 more in wages than Kerkhoff. But there was only $45,000 between the two bids. Bill Kerkhoff appeared to be pocketing an extra $581,000 on the project. This fascinating aspect of Bill Bennett's New Reality was not missed by the trade-union movement.

Fearing the worst, Jimmy Pattison was still trying to hammer out a deal with Gauthier and the Building Trades. On June 14, at 1:00 A.M., with the help of the new deputy minister of labour, Graham Leslie, Pattison and Gauthier arrived at an agreement: non-union workers on the Expo site would receive minimum union scale. Gauthier left to get his executive's approval of the deal, and Pattison said he would recommend it to his board. But he had trouble getting a quorum: too many federal Liberal appointees were off in Ottawa at the Liberal leadership convention. Gauthier got the approval, but Pattison failed after an eleven-hour board meeting.

The problem was Kerkhoff. His contract had already been let; he was moving equipment onto the site. If the wage agreement was retroactive, it would put his price above his nearest competitor. Jimmy told his board and Gauthier he would get a compromise from Kerkhoff for the good of the project.

Jimmy climbed into his red 1975 Pontiac convertible and slid onto the Trans-Canada Highway, heading east to Chilliwack for a meeting with Bill Kerkhoff. Just after he hit the highway, he glanced up and spotted the BCTV helicopter. A few miles further and the chopper was still there; Pattison was being tailed. BCTV had been tipped off that a deal was going down, and they wanted the pictures. When Jimmy got to the Chilliwack exit he turned south instead of north and pulled into the yard of his fruit-packing plant, Berryland. The BCTV helicopter lost him and set down at Kerkhoff's. Jimmy acted as though nothing was happening – he'd just stopped by to count his money. When Jimmy left Berryland and headed for Kerkhoff's, he passed the BCTV helicopter going to Berryland.

Nothing came from his meeting with Kerkhoff; but that night BCTV ran with the story that Expo and the Socreds had given in to the union demands. Jimmy first got the news when he wandered into an evening reception at Government House in Victoria – a going-away party for Dave Barrett – and encountered a somewhat disconcerted Bill Bennett. After a bit of *mano a mano* in a side room Bennett made it clear that nobody was giving in to the unions. Gauthier would not get a deal.

By the end of June, Kerkhoff was on the site, and union workers had been out for ten days straight. Kerkhoff had convinced Pattison and his board that Expo could be built totally by non-union labour. The spokesman for the union contractors, Chuck McVeigh of the Construction Labour Relations Association, suggested that, "Honest to God, this government must be insane." The local Socred sob-sister in the afternoon paper was telling Bennett to kill the fair – "It isn't fun any more" – and Jimmy Pattison was on his knees to Bennett to outlaw strikes and lock-outs at Expo "as soon as possible".

Bennett sent Labour Minister Bob McClelland to an Expo board meeting to twist arms. McClelland told them that all future non-union contractors would be required to pay their workers the "Canadian fair wage", which was a lot closer to what Gauthier wanted than what Kerkhoff was paying; but the wage rate would not apply to Kerkhoff's three-week-old agreement. After two hours, the board went along with McClelland and spent the next five hours trying to pull their budget back into shape. They chopped $56 million from the amusement-rides allowance.

Tension at the Expo site continued to build through the early part of August. On August 22, a new non-union contracting firm turned up, Marabella Pacific Enterprises Ltd., of which Ewald Rempel, who still savoured his trashed Ford truck and the battle for Pennyfarthing, was a half owner. The other half was owned by Elmer Verigin of Verigin Industries Ltd. Marabella's bid on a $4.7 million contract was $20,000 lower than a union firm's. When Marabella's equipment started to roll onto the site, union workers took a walk, and the Building Trades Council stomped off to the Labour Relations Board. They argued that Expo was a single site, and therefore their members had the right to invoke their non-affiliation clause and to strike.

Two days later, on August 24, Bill Bennett proclaimed the amendments to the labour code. Expo was divided into fourteen "economic development" projects. Every future contract let would go to cabinet and be declared by special order-in-council to be a separate economic development project until the fair's opening day on May 2, 1986. Union contractors were told that if they had three consecutive days of work stoppage, their contracts would be cancelled.

The trade-union movement limped away from the field of battle, located, isolated, and destroyed by the Tough Guy's New Reality.

12

SPAZZING OUT

By 1984, Bill Bennett's revolution had developed its own vocabulary, a neo-conservative Newspeak. He had renamed the private sector the "productive sector". People were no longer fired, they were "laid off". Social services were not gutted, but "downsized"; or sometimes they were not obliterated, but declared "desirable but not essential". The Solidarity skirmishes of the previous long summer and fall were over. The public service was dispirited. Half of Canada's food banks were in British Columbia, and they were turning people away. Bankruptcies and unemployment continued to soar well above the national averages.

While not all or even most of the blame for the lame economy could be hung around Bill Bennett's neck, what little influence the provincial government had was being exerted by the Socreds to drive the province further into recession. This was the assessment of the Conference Board of Canada. The privately funded group of conservative policy analysts concluded that Bennett's restraint program was causing consumer demand and business services to lag. Their board's chief provincial economist, Peter Gusen, observed that the B.C. consumer was "shell shocked". As the province braced itself for the next budget, no group dreaded the coming year more than the education sector: the teachers, the school boards, the parents, the students.

Richard and Donna Britton pick up their daughter, Vandy, from the Tsawassen ferry terminal south of Vancouver on Friday evening, September 28, 1984, and drive her the few miles to Delta Secondary School. The parking lot is full. The north gymnasium is filling up with parents and friends. This is graduation night. Cut flowers line the stage. The band, under the energetic direction of Rob Greenwood, is playing "Pomp and Circumstance" for the first of many times that evening.

Vandy is the valedictorian. She will be awarded a provincial government scholarship for coming in the top 3 per cent in the provincial government scholarship exams. (Delta Secondary picked up twice the provincial average of these scholarships.) As well, she will be awarded the Delta Cablevision Award for excellence in the arts; Vandy sings, acts, and plays in the school band. She will also take home the Delta Community Band Award, the University of Victoria President's Regional Award, and the Delta Teachers' Association Award for achievement by the son or daughter of a teacher in the district; her mother, Donna, teaches kindergarten at McCloskey Elementary.

Education Minister Jack Heinrich is a special guest, here to open phase one of Delta Secondary's building program. Phases two and three, a new theatre, a computer centre, and more offices, have been lost to restraint. Heinrich makes the opening remarks one would expect of a minister of education. Then Vandy takes the podium and begins her address.

The audience starts to fidget, and Heinrich takes agitated notes. Vandy has departed from the traditional platitudes and launched into an attack on Socred educational policy. "Because of our late graduation due to government exams, we must disrupt things temporarily to return to perform something that should have been done three months ago." A last-minute decision to reinstitute province-wide exams threw the system into a panic that only added to the disruption caused by endless government budget cutbacks.

"Perhaps the most encouraging thing about continuing

one's education is that it provides one with so many opportunities." She appears to be back on track. But then she continues, "It is a shame that many of these opportunities are disappearing because of higher tuition rates and limited enrolment in colleges and universities. It is discouraging to find doors closing in our faces as unemployment continues and funds are scarce; but we can turn these disappointments into advantages as we learn to face and overcome the obstacles thrown at us by the government and by life." At this point Vandy is aware of Heinrich sitting immediately behind her: "He was really spazzing out."

She goes on to quote William Lyon Mackenzie: "The attention paid to education in the United States is the grand secret of their power and the most indissoluble bond of their union." And she adds, "This is of especially grave concern in B.C., where the amount of money spent on education is lower than [in] any other province in Canada."

Heinrich leans over and whispers to Delta school superintendent Gerry Moulds, "How does she know all this?"

Moulds whispers back, "Her mother's a teacher."

Vandy's knees begin to knock, but she finishes the address. Heinrich is gone before she can talk to him.

In January 1984 Jack Heinrich sent a letter to all the community colleges and vocational institutions in the province. In part it read: "The ministry of education has been instructed by cabinet to reduce, and in some cases eliminate, programs within colleges/institutes that are or can be offered in the private sector." In this case the private sector was the Private Career Training Association of B.C., which had been lobbying for years through Labour Minister Bob McClelland, the minister responsible for apprenticeship training.

The net effect of this move would be to downsize or eliminate business and clerical courses, hairdressing courses, skin-care programs, and radio and television courses in community colleges. The lobbyists demanded a commitment from the Socreds for the same level of bursaries, loans, and grants to private-sector students that students in the public sector received.

There was a difference, however. Courses at private schools were vastly more expensive. Kids on the year-long waiting list to enrol in, say, the skin-care program at Vancouver City College would have to go instead to a private outfit. Instead of the $208 tuition at vcc, they would have to dish out $3,000 or more. The people affected were, of course, mostly those at the bottom of the ladder. People like vcc student Kelly Faraday, who explained that the publicly offered skin-care and hairdressing courses "are a way out for a lot of kids". That way out was closing.

David Thompson University Centre (DTUC) in Nelson was closing as well. It was the only degree-granting institution in the B.C. interior, an arts college that Bill Bennett opened in 1977. Six months before the Socreds announced the shutdown, Jack Heinrich had sent the centre's administration a glowing letter assuring them they would be continued. But times had changed. DTUC was no longer essential. One of the largest employers in the economically depressed town of Nelson would have to fire 150 staff members and kiss off 500 students. In B.C., a kid from the lower mainland stands twice as good a chance as an up-country kid of going on to post-secondary training. DTUC had been an attempt to correct that inequity. Now it was gone.

At the three remaining universities, tuition fees were being jacked up and enrolments were being restricted. The University of British Columbia led the way with a 33 per cent tuition-fee hike in anticipation of the budget. Federal funds for higher education were increasing, but they were siphoned off in Victoria for other things; Socreds actually cut funds to universities by 6 per cent.

Two years after the restraint program was launched, teachers were still being fired and courses shut down, as Victoria controlled budgets to force class sizes back up to 1976 levels. The government never explained what was so great about the quality of education in 1976, but it was the first full year in power for Bill Bennett and his Nouveau

Socreds. The government simply advanced the theory that you don't "necessarily" improve the quality of education by paying teachers more money and pumping more tax dollars into the system. Why not cut money from the system and see what happens?

A group of angry Surrey parents turned up at a Bill Bennett ribbon-cutting for an extension to the rapid-transit system to argue that education should have the same priority as transit. At least thirty-nine teaching positions were being eliminated in their district. The Tough Guy later told reporters that the protesters were "bad British Columbians", who didn't want the province to achieve success under a Social Credit government. Give them all black hats.

At Vandy Britton's alma mater in Delta, twelve teachers had been cut since restraint became the New Reality. Delta already boasted the lowest cost per pupil of any district in the province, but now funds were cut for school supplies, including such things as wood, food, metal, and guitar strings. There was no money for academic field trips, and athletic field trips were reduced, making it next to impossible to hold regular competitions. The school maintenance program was cut: repainting the buildings would have to wait another year. At Delta Secondary, as at most schools in the province, tension still existed between teachers who went out on the Solidarity strike in 1983 and those who had crossed the line.

In 1984 the Delta school board overran its budget by $635,321. Jack Heinrich said they would have to take that money out of the next year's budget. Then he decided to fine them $300,000 just to teach them a lesson. The school board announced that it would sell three schools to cover the shortfall. Heinrich finally relented and sent staff from Victoria to rejig the books, including giving credit for a federal grant of $113,000 the province had neglected to forward. The overrun was finally reduced to $168,000, which was largely caused by increased teacher absenteeism. There would be no penalty. Delta school board chairperson Mary Bittroff reported that "all seven of our board members were physically ill over this [fight with Victoria]." She added that "at the beginning of the restraint program we were told we would be rewarded for our good management. Instead, we were shot through the head."

The Monday after Vandy Britton delivered her valedictory address, the ministry of education began a quiet investigation. Heinrich talked to his deputy, Jim Carter, who phoned Delta superintendent Gerry Moulds, who got on the blower to Delta Secondary principal Colin Campbell. On the weekend Campbell had been quoted on the front page of the Vancouver *Sun* as saying that Vandy's address was "powerful". The superintendent told him that the deputy minister wanted to know the answer to a question raised by the minister: Was Jack Heinrich set up? Was this a plot to embarrass the Social Credit government, and was Colin Campbell in cahoots with the perpetrators of this nasty bit of business? Campbell told the superintendent that he wasn't in the habit of either screening or proofreading valedictory speeches. Not guilty.

The Socred budget in February 1984 was promoted as a fiscal landmark. For the first time since Wacky Bennett came to power in 1952, the people of B.C. would be presented with a budget in which the government planned to spend less money than in the previous year. The Socreds would spend less by eliminating all bursaries and grants for students, who would be offered repayable loans instead. Funding to public schools and post-secondary institutions would be chopped, as would funding for all government operations except for a few under the ministry of health.

The Socreds introduced a new standard by which services would be chopped. Finance Minister Hugh Curtis said they would be "services which British Columbians would wish to buy for themselves". The health budget would actually go up by $50 million; but this would be offset by a tax increase, a "temporary health-care maintenance surtax", which was blamed on Ottawa's allegedly having short-changed B.C. on transfer payments. In the first year, the tax would put almost $100 million into the provincial treasury. Not a bad profit: over five years it should generate considerably more than the alleged shortfall from Ottawa.

In the New Reality, incentives for people at the top of the heap were created through grants and tax cuts. For those at the bottom of the heap the incentive was provided by taking away money. One man's carrot is another man's stick. In the thousands of words of the budget speech announcing "the new economic reality", the word "unemployment" did not slip once from the minister of finance's lips. Speak no evil, see no evil. (B.C.'s unemployment rate was exceeded in North America only by those of Newfoundland and Virginia.) The Socreds then proceeded to outline the new incentive program for welfare recipients. (In the July 1983 budget all welfare rates were frozen, and a $50 per month work incentive, the Community Involvement Program for handicapped and "unemployable" welfare recipients, was phased out. It was resurrected in a more limited form, excluding "unemployables" in May 1984.).

Single people and childless couples under twenty-five were the first to get the chop: $50 for the first month, $25 a month for the next seven months. (The unemployment rate for this group was 24.2 per cent.) They were soon joined by people in that precarious position between their last paycheque and their first unemployment cheque or first instalment of Canada pension, who were only eligible for emergency income assistance. "Short-term assistance" – welfare at reduced rates for the first four months – would now be extended to the first eight months on the dole. The point of this tightening up, the Socreds said, was "to reduce the chances of creating permanent unemployed persons and attracting recipients from outside the province." Immigration to B.C. from all sources was one-tenth of its level four years earlier. The saving to the Socred treasury was $31.3 million in the first year.

The throne speech of the New Reality announced that British Columbia was "entering a new era of Human Rights where a greater emphasis will be placed on individual responsibility for eliminating discrimination." The new bill was virtually the same as the one that had tumbled down in the legislative avalanche on July 7, 1983, only to be abandoned in the Solidarity wars. Yet the debate during the passage of this new bill was even more acrimonious than the first time around.

The first hearing before the new Human Rights Council was a charge of sexual harassment. The complainant was a young waitress named Andrea Fields. Andrea had been in the restaurant business – starting as a bus girl in Calgary – since she was fourteen. She was nineteen when she moved to Victoria and started working for Wilhelm Ueffing at Willie's Rendezvous, a civil-service breakfast and lunch spot.

Willie's has the ambiance of a West Coast fern bar – hanging plants, cedar panelling, a muted indoor-outdoor carpet, and fifteen neat, rectangular arborite tables. The walls are covered with colour photos in thin metallic frames. There's a sunset, a shack in the woods, the rotting hull of a fish boat pulled up on the shore. But sprinkled among the nature shots are photos of women. One is in a fur coat with one breast drooping through the opening. Another woman is stretched out in a negligée having a smoke. A third sits naked, except for a headset, in an old-fashioned bathtub. Odd.

Andrea worked at Willie's for five and a half months. Almost from the start, she claimed, Ueffing, the owner, had his hands all over her, grabbing her breasts, pinching her, patting her ass. She'd say, "Cool it, Willie," or, "Keep your hands to yourself," but Willie carried right on, stealing a kiss, trapping her in a hug, sending her notes in a grade-school scrawl: "Darling Andrea – looking forward to seeing your sexy body again. Lots of luv." Or "Andrea, let's make love."

When Andrea finally left Willie's Rendezvous, she visited the new Human Rights Council to file a complaint of sexual harassment. Under the old legislation, which was tossed out along with the Human Rights Commission and most of the Human Rights Branch staff, Andrea's complaint would have been investigated by the Branch. If a hearing was required to resolve the issue, the Branch director would be party to the complaint along with Andrea. Branch staff would prepare a file on the investigation, and a lawyer with human-rights experience would be provided by the Branch to represent both the director and the complainant. The complainant wouldn't spend a cent. Under the new do-it-yourself system, in which "greater emphasis" is "placed on individual responsibility for eliminating discrimination", people like Andrea have to hunt up a lawyer, rustle up witnesses, and pay the bills – the equivalent of making a robbery victim responsible for prosecuting the thief.

By the time the case was heard on November 6, Andrea had Felix Reuben as her lawyer. Mr. Reuben was not considered a great authority on human-rights cases; Andrea was not very experienced in hunting up lawyers. The witness she tracked down was former worker, Rochelle Errett. She had worked for Willie while Andrea was ducking his advances. Rochelle said she had heard Andrea telling Willie to buzz off on more than one occasion. Rochelle was living with her mother when Andrea first approached her to be a witness. By the hearing date, however, Rochelle had moved in with her grandmother, and her mother's phone was out of order.

There is no court record of exactly what took place at the hearing, although journalists were present. The chairman of the hearing and head of the new Human Rights Council, Jim Edgett, could have authorized a transcript, but he passed on it to save money. Restraint. On the first day of the hearing, Andrea's lawyer, Reuben, apparently said he had no further witnesses, and Wilhelm Ueffing's lawyer started calling witnesses for Willie's case.

That night, after the hearing was temporarily adjourned, Andrea managed to track down Rochelle Errett at her grandmother's house and told her to come for the next scheduled day of the hearing, November 8. With Rochelle Errett in the hearing room, Andrea's lawyer tried to get her testimony introduced as evidence. There was a bit of toing and froing among Willie's lawyer, Andrea's lawyer, and Edgett, the chairman. Edgett was told the nature of the evidence but ruled against hearing it. Willie's lawyer then produced a handful of witnesses to tell the hearing what a nice affectionate guy old Willie was.

On November 22, Andrea Fields heard the outcome of her hearing on the radio, before the commission had informed her she'd lost. When "the smoke cleared", Jim Edgett, administering the "best human rights legislation in the country", decided that Andrea didn't have a case for sexual harassment. Edgett's ruling said: "It was obvious from the testimony of several witnesses that it was Mr. Ueffing's nature to warmly greet both his staff and regular customers with a hug and a kiss on the cheek . . . . such activity did not constitute sexual harassment."

As for Ms. Fields' testimony that she was grabbed and pinched, Edgett said: "There was no evidence that Mr. Ueffing ever pinched or grabbed various parts of Ms. Fields' anatomy (including her breasts) or that he attempted to do so, nor was there evidence other than the testimony of Miss Fields that Miss Fields objected to the alleged conduct of Mr. Ueffing." Those suggestive little notes could, Edgett concluded, "if taken out of context, be interpreted as being crude or offensive. However, it was clear from the evidence that Mr. Ueffing was a habitual, even compulsive, writer of notes." He does it to everybody. Case closed. Complaint dismissed.

Labour Minister Bob McClelland defended Edgett and attacked critics of Edgett's decision. They have a "pretty skewed idea of justice", he said. "I think there was a fair hearing and a decision made." He would not review the case. That was his prerogative under the new law.

(Bob McClelland was shuffled out of the Labour portfolio on February 27, 1985. On the eve of the shuffle he used the services of Top Hat Productions, a Victoria-based escort service that also arranges for strip-o-grams and exotic dancers. A short time later Victoria police raided Top Hat's premises and scooped up a number of documents, including a processed Visa slip in McClelland's name for $130. On May 6, 1985, police laid nineteen charges of procuring, facilitating, and living off the avails of prostitution against the head of Top Hat. B.C.'s Attorney General, Brian Smith, said the police found no evidence of criminal wrongdoing on McClelland's part. McClelland said, "I've hired the best libel lawyer in the country.")

Andrea Fields' only recourse was a narrow and expensive appeal to the Supreme Court of British Columbia. She and her lawyers could only argue an "error in law", and at best they would get another hearing before Edgett's council. Andrea hired a second firm of lawyers, with a better handle on this particular area of the law. The appeal was heard by Mr. Justice Makoff. His judgment was handed down on April 10, 1985. He was not impressed with Jim Edgett's abilities, and he was most interested in the evidence of Rochelle Errett.

> In her affidavit Ms. Errett deposed that the evidence she would be able to give, had she been permitted to do so, would be, *inter alia*:
> (a) that I personally witnessed Mr. Ueffing fondle, kiss, grab, pat "bottoms", and "hump" the petitioner, which advances I personally heard her object to constantly;
> (b) that I personally had experienced similar advances including patting my "bottom", kissing me, and hugging me.

Justice Makoff concluded that there were grounds for a judicial review.

Edgett's "refusal to hear cogent evidence resulted in a failure to comply with the requirements of natural justice. What Mr. Edgett did, and what he failed to do, was of such a nature that it makes his decision a nullity . . . . he refused to hear the evidence, even though, if accepted, it would prove [that Andrea Fields was sexually harassed]."

The Justice added:

> Mr. Edgett obviously attached great significance to the fact that, aside from the evidence of the complainant, there was no other evidence as to those various mat-

ters. The reason that there was no other evidence is that
he refused to hear it . . . . Having wrongly refused to
hear the proffered evidence, he then . . . went on to
draw an inference adverse to the complainant because
of its absence. A decision founded on such a breach of
fundamental justice cannot be permitted to stand. The
decision is therefore set aside and a new hearing ordered. In fairness to the parties and to Mr. Edgett, the
new hearing should be held before another [member of
the council].

Copies of the Edgett decision were distributed at the
November 1984 convention of the B.C. Federation of Labour as a painful reminder of the failure of the Kelowna
Accord to moderate the Socred position on human rights.
Promises of meaningful consultation came to nothing. And
the legacy of the living-room arrangement worked out between Bill Bennett and Jack Munro was prominent as well
in the power struggle going on for the election of federation
officers.

To see Art Kube, Joy Langan, and the BCGEU's Jack
Adams on the convention stage you would think you were
at a recruiting rally for Weight Watchers. Add to the tab-
leau Jack Munro's six-foot-four-inch frame – twenty-five
pounds heavier since he quit drinking and smoking – and
you couldn't help but see these figures as a metaphor for
their movement. It was aging, out of shape, and sloppy; it
was up against a lean, tough, tanned, tennis-playing
Bennett.

The central battle at the BCFed convention was an attempt to unload Art Kube. Munro was determined to replace him with Joy Langan, a journeyman printer and vice-
president of the provincial NDP. Munro spent the week
before the convention lining up votes for Langan and bad-
mouthing Kube's lack of leadership. The other contender
was Frank Kennedy, the head of the Vancouver Labour
Council and godfather of left-wing politics in the city.
Kube planned to come up the middle with backing from the
B.C. Government Employees' Union.

The people backing Kube were not the only ones intent on knocking off Munro. The Kelowna Accord had added to Munro's already substantial list of enemies in the labour movement. Many were already angry with him for his stand against secondary picketing and non-affiliation clauses. He was, in the words of Jack Adams, "a dinosaur". He was part of a fading force being pushed aside by public-sector unions, who were more militant in their dealings with governments, interested in more than the traditional bread-and-butter issues, and more open to the demands of women, the handicapped, and environmentalists.

Mike Kramer, the noisy BCFed secretary-treasurer who had been forever threatening a "rumble" during the Solidarity protests, was in the Munro camp. Kube naively tried to cut a deal to keep Munro and Kramer on the executive. The day before the vote he was so frustrated by his inability to pull the convention together that he broke down and cried. Munro consoled him. On the day of the vote Kube had passing thoughts of just giving up and walking away from it.

When the votes were counted Kube beat out his opponents, but it took two ballots. Munro and Kramer were out. Kramer was replaced by the smooth, bright, sophisticated chief negotiator from the BCGEU, Cliff Andstein. Munro was replaced by his arch enemy in the pulp unions, Art Gruntman. When it was all over Munro lamely joked, "Art's got the votes, but I've still got the press." When Munro lost, the IWA refused to run any members for the federation executive and, a few weeks later, like children in a spat over a game of marbles, they pulled most of their funding from the organization and went away to sulk. In the spring of 1985, Jack Munro was given an honorary Doctor of Laws degree by the University of British Columbia.

Dave Barrett was still sliding into bottomless pools of self-pity one and a half years after his third election defeat at the hands of Bill Bennett. He did not want to talk about Bill Bennett, the 1983 election, the legislative avalanche that followed, or his humbling and historic ejection from the legislature. Instead, he launched into a tirade against an uncaring government, a hypocritical business community – "If Bill Bennett didn't exist they would invent him" – and an equally contemptuous media that never took the NDP seriously.

Just look, he said, as he jabbed a pudgy finger in the air and launched an assault on Bill Bennett's megaprojects: Expo 86 "with its $450-million dollar deficit"; ALRT, the rapid-transit system, with more than a billion dollars in bills and no plans for who would pay the shot; and north-east coal, a megaproject that could, arguably, cost more jobs than it would create. And what economists had ever examined critically what the government had done to the economy?

"I'll just play the role: Fat, Happy Dave; very moderate," he said. And then he turned his attention to the man to whom he most clearly owed the style he adopted in his brief three years as premier. Wacky Bennett. It all seemed to be reduced to one searing memory, of "that old man calling me a fat little Jew boy." Through his years in politics Barrett nurtured his own sugar-coated recollection of that comment, referring to himself as "Fat Little Dave" on the campaign trail.

Then he repeated: "I'm not ready to talk."

Polarization has only deepened since Bennett returned to power in 1983. The grinding, bitter divisions he helped promote – between the Socreds and the "bad British Columbians" or the "coalition of dissent", between public- and private-sector workers, between unions and their leadership – permeate life in the province. You need go no further than a quick check of the personal columns:

> WHISTLER/PEMBERTON AREA bi-male seeks
> healthy, straight-acting man for winter
> sports and cultural activities. No Socreds.
> Reply Box 8092 c/o West Ender.

The Tough Guy's New Reality was tested at the polls in two by-elections at the beginning of November 1984. In Vancouver East, Fat Little Dave was finally being replaced; in Okanagan North, a few miles up the valley from Kelowna, the incumbent insignificant Socred backbencher had passed away a few months earlier. It was also the first test for Bob Skelly, the new leader of the NDP. Skelly was the new generation on the left. He brought with him a high-tech approach to politics, The Pink Machine, which viewed confrontation as a weakness that only played to the Tough Guy's strength.

Vancouver East was a sure win for the NDP, but Okanagan North had been a Socred stronghold for as long as there had been Socreds in the legislature, more than thirty years. Eight days before the by-election the Socreds announced a $10-million road-construction program in Okanagan North. The Socreds still lost by more than 3,000 votes.

Throughout the campaign, Bill Bennett was nowhere to be seen. He was in California with his Kelowna buddies playing tennis under orders from his political geneticist, Patrick Kinsella. In Kinsella's Tough Guy lecture to the Simon Fraser University Student Marketing Association he explained the loss in Okanagan North.

> Bill Bennett didn't show up in [the riding] . . . because I told him not to go. And the reason he didn't go is because the polls said that he would be a wash. Not a negative, not a positive . . . . Public-sector restraint really didn't matter to them one way or the other . . . . That wasn't a big issue for them. But what they were concerned about was a kind of a lack of feeling, you know, that government cares. That government cares about you and cares about the people in Okanagan North . . . .
>
> On the Monday before the election I had a business meeting with several businessmen in Vernon, and they gave me that same feeling. Well, we're not so sure we're going to vote. We got to send the guy a message.

What is the message going to say? You know, we're just not happy. We're not feeling good about ourselves . . . .

You know, in the last [Decima Research] quarterly, when we looked at it from province to province to province, British Columbia is the only province in which when you ask this question: How do you feel personally about the future? Are you optimistic or are you pessimistic? Not your future but the future of . . . your province – British Columbia is the only province in the Dominion that says it's pessimistic . . . .

They sent a message to Bill Bennett. That's traditionally the story of a by-election . . . . And they did it in spades. And the true test of all of that will be whether or not Bill Bennett responds to that message. And I'll guarantee as I sit down that he will, because I'm going to have a poll to tell him how to do it.

Shortly after that lecture, the "best political hack in the country" headed east to work for Larry Grossman in the Ontario Conservative leadership race and then to run Frank Miller's machine in the next provincial election.

During the next few weeks and months Bennett tried to modify his image and market the Love in his Tough Love strategy. The polls said people want a caring government. Bennett would care. In an interview with the *Globe and Mail* in March he gave his defence to the criticism that he had run a mean administration: "To suggest we have been mean over those three years by anyone . . ." he said sharply before catching himself. "One only has to look that we are still running a deficit of nearly a billion dollars. That is still a debt we must pay. I think a government that has only the balance sheet in mind would not achieve the sort of balance that we have."

The alchemy is complete. The deficit, that single symbol that motivated first Wacky Bennett and then his son Bill, was there to be used still. A decade earlier the deficit was an icon, sure sign of socialist profligacy. In the recession of the early eighties the deficit was transformed into a threat to a secure British Columbian future, a "severe fiscal imbalance" caused by a world economy gone sour. Now it had been genetically engineered into something quite different – not an outside threat but a statement of caring and the measure of a Tough Guy's heart.

A Late Dispatch

As the war enters its third year, Bad British Columbians continue to be drawn into battle and are bitter in defeat. The win-lose imperative of Bill Bennett's Tough Love politics drains vital energies from a province that can ill afford it. Even Jim Matkin, spokesman for business and the architect of the Socred restraint program, is forced to complain that the Socreds "have a crisis management [approach] about them, and that creates a confrontational atmosphere that's not good for business."

At 8:00 A.M. on May 6, 1985, Bill Bennett's minister of education, Jack Heinrich, kicked the Vancouver school board out of power and into the streets. Less than a year into their two-year mandate, the nine-member board were replaced by a trustee. Unloading the Vancouver board was the climax of a battle between the Socreds and the province's school boards over cuts to education funding and the erosion of their autonomy.

The protest that evening on the school-board office steps drew only a few hundred people – more a groan of despair than the roar of rage that followed the July 1983 budget. BCFed president Art Kube said that large protests only draw people to the government's side. Heinrich said, "It is important that the rule of law must be obeyed."

A Vancouver *Sun* poll conducted in the lower mainland immediately afterward determined that people opposed the Socreds' action against the Vancouver school board by close to a two-to-one margin. An even greater margin believed that education was being underfunded.

The Vancouver school board was one of thirty-four school boards (out of a possible seventy-five) that had initially refused to comply with the government's financing formula to reduce funding for the 1985-86 school year, although during the weeks leading up to the May 1, 1985, deadline for budget submission the opposition had crumbled; the Vancouver board and only four others – Courtenay, Burnaby, Coquitlam, and Cowichan – had refused to submit restraint budgets. (In the end Courtenay, Burnaby, and Coquitlam capitulated, and on May 13 Jack Heinrich placed the Cowichan school district under trusteeship.)

During the days before the deadline, the president of the B.C. School Trustees' Association, Bill Lefeaux-Valentine, and members of the five hold-out boards asked for meetings with Bennett and Education Minister Jack Heinrich, but no meetings were agreed to. Tough Guys don't negotiate.

Lefeaux-Valentine resigned as president of the BCSTA and quit his post on the Queen Charlotte Islands school board, saying: "I can no longer honestly take a role in the destruction of public education." (A number of other trustees across the province, the president of UBC, and the head of the University of Victoria engineering school, also resigned.)

In the government's mind, the extreme polarization it had encouraged was now immutable. Heinrich said the aim of the left-of-centre majority of the Vancouver school board was "to defeat the government".

At a public meeting at the Vancouver board's offices, called by the Socred trustee, an unrepentant, deposed chairman, Pauline Weinstein, wondered aloud. What calibre of work would the trustee perform during the next year and a half? she asked him – that is, "If you live that long."

Bibliography

Books

Cohen, Dian, and Kristin Shannon. *The Next Canadian Economy.* Montreal: Eden Press, 1984.

Friedman, Milton, and Rose Friedman. *The Tyranny of the Status Quo.* San Diego, Calif.: Harcourt Brace Jovanovich, 1983.

Mitchell, David J. *W.A.C. Bennett and the Rise of British Columbia.* Vancouver: Douglas and McIntyre, 1983.

Newman, Peter C. *The Acquisitors.* Volume Two of *The Canadian Establishment.* Toronto: Seal Books, 1982.

Olson, Mancur. *The Rise and Decline of Nations.* New Haven, Conn.: Yale University Press, 1982.

Robin, Martin. *Pillars of Profit: The Company Province, 1934-1972.* Toronto: McClelland and Stewart, 1973.

Sheppard, Robert, and Michael Valpy. *The National Deal: The Fight for a Canadian Constitution.* Toronto: Macmillan of Canada, 1982.

Sherman, Paddy. *Bennett.* Toronto: McClelland and Stewart, 1966.

Periodicals

Annesley, Pat. "Tell 'em Billy Boy is here". *Equity,* April 1984.

Annesley, Pat. "Bill Bennett". *Equity,* May/June 1984.

Bennett, Bill. "Beginnings". *Today,* August 9, 1980.

Collins, Doug. "Big cat in the hat". *Equity,* May/June 1984.

Gourley, Catherine. "Union jackhammer". *Vancouver,* June 1984.

Govier, Katherine. "Polling Allan Gregg". *Toronto Life*, July 1985.

Ladner, Peter. "Who are those masked men?" *Vancouver*, January 1984.

Mason, Gary. "Weekend in Kelowna". *Vancouver*, June 1984.

Mitchell, Donald. Interview with Audrey Bennett. *Equity (Fall 1985, forthcoming).*

Index